A Grateful Response to God's Abundant Gifts

Stewardship in the Diocese of Wichita

Rev. C. Jarrod Lies

ISBN-10: **1986027449**
ISBN-13: **978-1986027441**

TO DAVID AND PATTY LIES

For giving me life,
sustaining me in love,
encouraging me to achieve,
accompanying me every day,
teaching me by word and example,
interceding for me to Mary and Joseph,
introducing me to the Father, Son, and Holy Spirit,
And guiding me to gratefully respond to God's abundant gifts.

Table of Contents

ACKNOWLEDGMENTS

Thank you to the faculty, staff and administration of the School of Theology of Sacred Heart Major Seminary, Detroit, Michigan for administrating the Licentiate in Sacred Theology (S.T.L.) for the New Evangelization. Thank you also to all the professors who prayed for and taught me throughout this program:

Dr. Eduardo J. Echeverria
Dr. Patricia Cooney Hathaway
Dr. Mary Healy
Dr. Daniel Keating
Dr. Ralph Martin
Dr. John McDermott, S.J.
Dr. Edward Peters
Dr. Ilaria L.E. Ramelli
Dr. Janet E. Smith
Dr. Peter S. Williamson

Special thanks to Dr. Peter S. Williamson who served as my thesis director.

A Stewardship Prayer

Help us Lord,

So that we would hold nothing back,

That no sacrifice would be too great, too costly, or too unthinkable.

Send us, Lord, heroes and heroines of stewardship,

Saints on the journey

Whose walk as disciples

Inspire us to imitate and pattern our own lives after.

Put on our path, Lord, men, women, and children

Who will model for us – for our diocese –

How to live, how to serve,

How to love the Lord with all our hearts.

Let this be our prayer,

Let this be our greatest desire and intention.[1]

- Bishop Carl Kemme, Bishop of the Diocese of Wichita

[1] Catholic Diocese of Wichita. *Stewarding our Gifts: Annual Parish Stewardship Renewal Planning Guide 2016/2017* (Wichita, KS: Catholic Diocese of Wichita, 2016), 2.

Chapter 1 - Introduction

God is so good! Indeed, all goodness is the overflowing abundance of God's graciousness. As St. James says, "All good giving and every perfect gift is from above, coming down from the Father of lights" (1:17, NABRE). God's abundance is a flood of generosity that calls forth gratitude returned in self-gift. Thus the Diocese of Wichita defines stewardship as *the grateful response of a Christian disciple who recognizes and receives God's gifts and shares these gifts in love of God and neighbor.*[2] As one pioneer of stewardship, Msgr. Thomas McGread, stated, "A stewardship way of life is a thanksgiving way of life, living life as God intended it to be lived."[3] He repeatedly said, "It's not a program. It's a way of life. And this is really the biggest mistake many people make."[4] The mistake referred to is reducing the idea of stewardship to financial development. In the Diocese of Wichita the accent of stewardship is on gratitude for God's gifts, not on methods of increased financial giving. Justin Clements, a current author on stewardship, agrees, "Stewardship is not fundraising. Rather, it is about a total way of life, about changing peoples' minds and hearts."[5] This change of mentality includes subordinating stewardship to discipleship and making discipleship missionary in practice.[6]

The goal of this paper is to summarize and explain the purpose and meaning of stewardship as practiced in the Diocese of Wichita. After an overview of its historical development within the diocese we will proceed through stewardship's scriptural, magisterial, and pastoral foundations and conclude with the identity and responsibilities of a steward. Although the foundations of stewardship will be explained, a detailed description

---

[2] Throughout this paper the title "Diocese of Wichita" is often abbreviated to "Wichita". This abbreviation refers to the entire corpus of documentation from which the meaning a spirituality of stewardship is described. The specific document referenced is found in the accompanying footnote.

[3] Deacon Donald R. *McArdle, Grateful and Giving, Grateful and Giving: How Msgr. Thomas McGread's Stewardship Message has Impacted Catholic Parishes throughout the Country* (Evans, GA: Catholic Stewardship Consultants, 2011), 9.

[4] Msgr. Thomas McGread, "A Foundation for Stewardship," YouTube video, 8:31, posted by the Catholic Diocese of Wichita, January 27, 2017, accessed August 8, 2017. https://www.youtube.com/watch?v=jFdMyFRz3H8.

[5] Justin C. Clements, *Time, Talent, and Treasure: Reflections on the U.S. Bishops' Model for Parish Stewardship* (Ligouri, MO: Ligouri Publications), Kindle Locations 125-126.

[6] Bishop Gerber speaks to this change of mentality, "Stewardship… is a grace, a conversion, a different way of viewing both visible and invisible realities. Attitudes shift, motivations change, relationships with God and with others become more life giving. 'Being more' outstrips 'having more.' People become more important than things and the loving awareness of God's presence becomes the treasure in the field and the pearl of great price." Most Rev. Eugene J. Gerber, "Human Love in the Divine Plan" (Paper presented at the Diocesan Stewardship Conference in the Diocese of Cheyenne, WY, January 18-20, 2005), 18.

of the process by which it is implemented within a parish is outside the scope of this paper.[7] A further aim of this paper is to elucidate the intrinsic relationship between stewardship, discipleship, and evangelization. Finally, it is hoped that persons more inclined to see stewardship in terms of finances will come to understand it more in terms akin to the apostolate as set forth in the documents of Vatican II. In view of these aims it is important to have four definitions in mind:

- *Stewardship* is: the grateful response of a Christian disciple who recognizes and receives God's gifts and shares these gifts in love of God and neighbor.

- A *steward* is: "One who receives God's gifts gratefully, cherishes and tends them in a responsible and accountable manner, shares them in justice and love with others, and returns them with increase to the Lord."[8]

- A *disciple* is: "One who responds to Christ's call, follows Jesus, and shapes his or her life in imitation of Christ's."[9]

- *Evangelization* is: "The proclamation of Christ and his Gospel by word and the testimony of life, in fulfillment of Christ's command."[10]

A Brief History of Stewardship in the Diocese of Wichita

Just as a fish tank needs a delicately balanced environment for fish to thrive the Diocese of Wichita provided the right environment for stewardship to thrive in the years immediately following Vatican II. The ingredients for this balance were fourfold: inspired pastors, highly engaged lay leadership, visionary Bishops, and a collaborative presbyterate. Lay movements, such as Marriage Encounter and the charismatic movement,

---

[7] I have however included some appendices at the end of this paper as helpful resources in this regard.

[8] United States Conference of Catholic Bishops, *Stewardship: A Disciple's Response: A Pastoral Letter on Stewardship. Tenth Anniversary Edition* includes *To Be a Christian Steward: A Summary of the U.S. Bishops' Pastoral Letter on Stewardship* and *Stewardship and Development in Catholic Dioceses and Parishes: a Resource Manual* (Washington, D.C.: United States Conference of Catholic Bishops, 2002), 9. Much recognition must be given to the Bishop's document entitled *Stewardship: A Disciple's Response* from which two of these definitions are taken.[8] It is an excellent exposition of the spirituality of stewardship on the national level. While I use this document as a primary source I strongly encourage it to be read. Its approach reflects the national characteristic of stewardship in the United States while this paper is concerned stewardship as it has been adapted by Wichita.

[9] Ibid.

[10] Catholic Church, *Catechism of the Catholic Church, 2nd ed.* (Washington, DC: United States Catholic Conference, 2000), glossary.

produced highly motivated leadership that provided the seedbed for stewardship to flourish. Msgr. Robert

Hemberger, former Vicar General of the diocese, said that these movements heralded "the awakening of a

sleeping giant among the laity... They were more than simple adult education they were also spiritual

formation."[11]

At the same time, in the year 1959, a young priest by the name of Fr. Thomas McGread was looking for a

new way to engage parishioners in the life of a parish. McGread, having been inspired by Fr. Joseph Jennings

and Fr. David Sullivan, recalls,

> They were trying to come up with a Catholic theology for the protestant idea of tithing... one of the
> things I noticed in their writings was that there was a tremendous emphasis on the fact that people are
> looking for standards in life... If we're looking for standards in life we also must be looking for standards
> in our relationship with God...I realized there must be more to this idea of building a relationship with
> God. So that's when I came up with the idea that all of us have a certain amount of time in this world,
> and all of us have a certain amount of talents.[12]

Armed with this conviction McGread took this message to four parishes within ten years from 1958-1968 until

he was made pastor of St. Francis of Assisi in West Wichita. It was in this parish where stewardship spread its

wings as it is practiced today in Wichita.[13] A history of stewardship in Wichita stated, "Msgr. McGread's

message was simple: strive to share our gifts of time, talent, and treasure for the service of God and all of His

people. Do this out of thanksgiving for all that He has given us."[14] Knowing people were striving for standards,

McGread put those standards squarely in front of them. With the persistence of "a steady drum beat" he

encouraged his parishioners to "give time to spouse, to family, God, and parish."[15] In the 1960's St. Francis of

Assisi parish was on the verge of closing its school. It was in this environment that McGread first proposed the

idea of Catholic schools as an extension of the parish mission with no tuition. Then, in the 1970's, the same

parish was burgeoning with good income and a growing population. Simple mathematics coupled with highly

---

[11] Msgr. Robert Hemberger, *A History of Stewardship in the Diocese of Wichita* (Wichita, KS: Catholic Diocese of Wichita, circa 2003), audio.

[12] McArdle, *Grateful and Giving,* 13-15.

[13] "It was there, within the life of that "normal" parish family, that the idea of living discipleship through the practice of stewardship was first understood, embraced, and modeled in this renowned stewardship diocese" (McArdle, *Grateful and Giving,* 6).

[14] Catholic Diocese of Wichita, *The History of Stewardship in the Diocese of Wichita* (Wichita, KS: Catholic Diocese of Wichita, date unknown), 1.

[15] Hemberger, audio.

engaged parishioners made the decision to go to tuition-free Catholic education, in both grade school and high school, easier to adopt.[16]

Then, later in the same decade, on the other side of town, Msgr. Bill Regan successfully presented this way of life to the Church of the Magdalen. It was a historically important moment, as Hemberger relates, "It showed that the theology, spirituality, and practice of stewardship was bigger than Fr. Tom McGread or some special charisma that he had or just the favorable demographics at St. Francis."[17]

About the same time Bishop Eugene J. Gerber, originally a priest of the Diocese of Wichita, returned to Wichita from Dodge City. As a priest of Wichita he witnessed the development of the stewardship way of life, its effects on people and parishes, and its blessings for the diocese as a whole. Returning as its Bishop, he joined McGread as one of the pioneers of this way of life both within the diocese as well as nationally. In 1985 two key events took place: *A People Gathered*, a series of diocesan listening sessions, and *Emmaus*, a convocation of priests. Concurrently new lay movements were again stirring in the diocese, specifically Cursillo and perpetual adoration. The confluence of these events created a new environment of engaged lay people, now coupled with a motivated presbyterate. The decision was then made for the entire diocese to adopt stewardship as a way of life under the title of *United Catholic Stewardship*. It took twenty five years to arrive at the fruits we will now discuss. Yet, stewardship is in a new generation. A new understanding needs to be articulated. A new flame needs to burst forth.

The Fruits of Stewardship in the Diocese of Wichita[18]

The value of stewardship in the Diocese of Wichita can be appreciated by considering its fruit (see Mt 7:16). Stewardship is a way of life, not a program. As a way of life it is an intrinsic aspect of discipleship and the fruits of stewardship are not separate from the lives of disciples.[19] In other words, stewardship is a property

---

[16] Ibid.

[17] Ibid.

[18] It must be admitted that there is a danger of speaking of the fruits so early in such a paper as this. Many people, having a financial understanding of stewardship, often seek the ostensible benefits first. But it must be kept in mind that the fruits about to be described have only come after almost fifty years of effort, much conversion, countless sacrifices, and many hard conversations.

[19] Not understanding this is the fatal mistake of so many parishes or dioceses that have sought to implement stewardship. Stewardship is not about the production of things. It is about the life of discipleship.

belonging to persons, not a production of things. When disciples are in love with God and neighbor they provide for each other out of grateful generosity. As such, the primary fruits of stewardship are always personal - both with God and with neighbor.

Preeminent among all the fruits of stewardship is that of the worship of God. According to the 2015 and 2016 October Mass counts, Mass attendance across the Diocese of Wichita was 47%, which is twice the national average.[20] Eucharistic adoration is a major part of the spirituality of parishioners. *A History of Stewardship in Wichita* observes, "63 of the 90 parishes have some sort of adoration opportunities."[21] Over thirty of those parishes have perpetual adoration. St. Francis of Assisi has had perpetual adoration for 31 years. Gerber states, "I believe that the fruits of stewardship in the parish and home have intertwined with Eucharistic Adoration."[22] Both of these facts have resulted in a per capita number of vocations to the priesthood that is significantly higher than the national average. Wichita, a diocese of one hundred and twenty thousand Catholics, had twenty-four seminarians in 1993, thirty-five seminarians in 2005, and forty-six seminarians in 2017. In 2017 ten men were ordained to the priesthood. Another ten men will be ordained in 2018. In addition, the total Catholic population growth is also greater than the state average. From 2000-2010 the Catholic population grew by 17.7% while the rest of the state Catholic population grew by 5.1%.[23]

Stewardship's effect on the love of neighbor is seen most explicitly in increased solidarity both among parishioners and among priests. In 1969 the parishioners of St. Francis were "more a collection of cliques than a unified parish."[24] So too, when Bishop Gerber returned to Wichita as Bishop, he found the priests "divided down the middle."[25] Gerber states that a fruit of stewardship was "a greater spirit and an overall all unity within our parishes as a diocese" as well as "...our greatest strength [being] the unity, the morale and the support of priests for one another."[26] This solidarity is further seen in the increase of ministries within stewardship

---

[20] Lois Loicey, "Stewardship and Evangelization" (paper presented at ICSC 2015, October, 23, 2015).

[21] CDOWK, *History*, 3.

[22] Gerber, *Human Love*, 29.

[23] Fred Mann, "Catholics, Mormons see most growth in Wichita and Kansas," *The Wichita Eagle*, May 7, 2012, accessed August, 14, 2017, http://www.kansas.com/news/article1091733.html.

[24] McArdle, *Grateful and Giving,* 25.

[25] Most Rev. Eugene J. Gerber, phone interview, July 25th, 2017.

[26] CDOWK, *History*, 3.

parishes. At St. Francis of Assisi there are over one hundred and fifty six (156) articulated service opportunities currently active.[27] There is also increased youth commitment, including youth service opportunities.[28] Also, *A History of Stewardship in Wichita* observes, "diocesan ministries have been created and overwhelmingly been supported: Guadalupe Clinic (40 doctors, 3000 patients); The Lord's Diner (6,500 volunteers, 2,500 meals served per night); Catholic Care Center" as well as the Harbor House women's shelter and the Anthony Family Shelter for struggling families.[29]

There are visible physical benefits as well. "In 1985 the combined annual diocesan income of all the parishes was under 15 million. By 2014, that income was over $51 million."[30] At St. Francis of Assisi, the average giving per registered household in 2017 was $1777.00 per household while the national average of the same year was $455.00.[31] Due to *United Catholic Stewardship* there are no cathedraticums, annual appeals, and only two special collections. Also, Wichita is the only diocese in the world where all active stewards who seek to go to Catholic grade or high schools can do so without tuition. This includes over 11,000 students, with Catholic schools opening, not closing (as is the national trend), and others expanding.[32] One such school is a rural parish with one hundred and forty five (145) families but with a school of one hundred and eighty five (185) students, supported entirely by stewardship.

A Brief Inter-Parochial Comparative Study

Stewardship as a way of life has been adopted by many parishes throughout the United States. Parishes that adopt this way of life report increases in parish ministries, outreach to the needy, perpetual adoration, RCIA membership, offertory, volunteerism, planned giving, and communication.[33] Fr. David Zimmer, pastor of St. John the Apostle in Bismark, ND, states, "We have become more prayerful, joyful, helpful people."[34] Charles

---

[27] St. Francis of Assisi Parish, *2017 Stewardship Time and Talent Adult Form* (Wichita, KS: Catholic Diocese of Wichita, 2017). This number includes 15 new service opportunities added in the 2017 calendar year.

[28] St. Francis of Assisi Parish, *Stewardship: Living Life as God Intended It* (Wichita, KS: St. Francis of Assisi Parish, 2004) 15.

[29] CDOWK, *History*, 3.

[30] Ibid.

[31] Loicey, 2.

[32] McArdle, *Grateful and Giving,* 62. J.J. Ziegler, "The State of Catholic Schools in the US," *The Catholic World Report*, May 31, 2011, accessed August 14, 2017. http://www.catholicworldreport.com/2011/05/31/the-state-of-catholic-schools-in-the-us/.

[33] McArdle, *Grateful and Giving,* 83-94; 129-143.

Zech in his book *Best Practices in Parish Stewardship* compares two hundred and twenty seven (227) stewardship parishes to two hundred and eight (208) non-stewardship parishes.[35] He discovered that "those parishes that demonstrate their commitment to stewardship by placing it at the heart of their parish plan receive significantly greater levels of all four of our stewardship measures."[36] These four measures are:

1. Treasure (regular contribution per household),

2. Volunteering (percent of parishioners actively volunteering),

3. Spiritual Index (percent of parishioners regularly attended a weekday Mass, adoration/rosary, Bible studies. small group retreats, or small faith groups),

4. Parish outreach (average number of outreach programs supported by parish). [37]

The average increase found within stewardship parishes over the national average ranged anywhere from 10% to 31% in each of these areas[38]. The following table compares the national average of all parishes studied to parishes identified as stewardship parishes and to St. Francis of Assisi parish in Wichita.

	National Average	Average of Stewardship Parishes	St. Francis of Assisi in Wichita, KS in 2017
Treasure	$517 per household	$656 per household	$1777 per household
Volunteering	27% of parishioners	32.13% of parishioners	39% of parishioners
Spiritual Index	46.3% of parishioners	59.7% of parishioners	----
Parish Outreach	3.34 per parish	4.6 per parish	10 at SFA

As Charles Zech has illustrated, the stewardship way of life has clear markers of success.

---

[34] McArdle, *Grateful and Giving*, 103.
[35] Charles E. Zech, *Best Practices in Parish Stewardship* (Huntington: Our Sunday Visitor, 2008), 16.
[36] Ibid., 71
[37] Ibid., 28-31.
[38] Taken from tables found on pages 48, 57, 62, 74, 86, 95, 105.

Chapter 2 - The Textbook of Stewardship

As lava churns in the heart of the earth, so the Word of God should churn in the heart of the Christian.

Stewardship is biblically rooted, and the stewardship way of life is nourished by contemplation on the Word of

God. As Vatican II exhorts the faithful,

> The sacred synod also earnestly and especially urges all the Christian faithful…to learn by frequent reading of the divine Scriptures the "excellent knowledge of Jesus Christ" (Phil. 3:8). "For ignorance of the Scriptures is ignorance of Christ." Therefore, they should gladly put themselves in touch with the sacred text itself (Dei Verbum, 25).

Wichita teaches that "the textbook for Christian stewardship is the holy Bible."[39] And McGread repeatedly

taught, "We must saturate ourselves with the scriptures. We must read and reflect on them regularly, and then

go and live them out."[40]

Foundations of Stewardship in the Old Testament

Image of God: Genesis 1:26-31

[26] Then God said: Let us make human beings in our image, after our likeness. Let them have dominion over the fish of the sea, the birds of the air, the tame animals, all the wild animals, and all the creatures that crawl on the earth. [27] God created mankind in his image; in the image of God he created them; male and female he created them. [28] God blessed them and God said to them: Be fertile and multiply; fill the earth and subdue it. Have dominion over the fish of the sea, the birds of the air, and all the living things that crawl on the earth. [29 n] God also said: See, I give you every seed-bearing plant on all the earth and every tree that has seed-bearing fruit on it to be your food; [30] and to all the wild animals, all the birds of the air, and all the living creatures that crawl on the earth, I give all the green plants for food. And so it happened. [31] God looked at everything he had made, and found it very good.

"God created mankind in his image; in the image of God he created them" (Gen 1:27). Out of nothing

(*ex nihilo*) God created everything. Everything created is a gift. Pope St. John Paul II writes, "Man appears in

creation as one who has received the world as a gift."[41] God's nature is to give.[42] Just as it is intrinsic to God's

identity to give, so too, we who are created "in his image" (v. 27) are called to give. Creation is an aspect of

---

[39] Catholic Diocese of Wichita, *The Formation of Christian Stewards: A Parish Stewardship Council Handbook* (Wichita, KS: Catholic Diocese of Wichita, June 2009), 18. McArdle, *Grateful and Giving,* 18.

[40] McGread, May 12th, 2011, in Catholic Stewardship Consultants, Inc. Blog, accessed, August 8, 2017, http://www.catholicsteward.com/category/msgr-mcgread/page/2/.

[41] Pope St. John Paul II, *Man and Woman He Created Them: A Theology of the Body*, trans. M. Waldstein (Boston, MA: Pauline Books & Media, 2006), 181.

[42] The phrase "God gives" occurs over 60 times in the Old Testament.

God's self-communication so that through creation we might come to communion with the Creator. In describing the Orthodox Christian concept of stewardship Robert Holet says, "The whole of creation was a manifestation of the providential and intimate love of God and intended as a means through which humans could commune with God in love, thanksgiving, and joy."[43]

Furthermore, God bequeathed on human persons "dominion" (vv. 26, 28) over all animals and plants. The *Catechism of the Catholic Church* (CCC) states, "In the beginning God entrusted the earth and its resources to the common stewardship of mankind to take care of them, master them by labor, and enjoy their fruits. The goods of creation are destined for the whole human race" (2402). Stewardship presupposes the universal destination of goods which obliges persons to put their possessions at the service of their neighbor. As God bestowed all created goods upon human persons, so too, those same persons are to share those goods with one another as stewards. [44]

Made for Communion: Genesis 2:7-24

[7] Then the LORD God formed the man out of the dust of the ground and blew into his nostrils the breath of life, and the man became a living being. [8] The LORD God planted a garden in Eden, in the east, and placed there the man whom he had formed. [9] Out of the ground the LORD God made grow every tree that was delightful to look at and good for food, with the tree of life in the middle of the garden and the tree of the knowledge of good and evil. [10] A river rises in Eden to water the garden; beyond there it divides and becomes four branches…. [12] The gold of that land is good; bdellium and lapis lazuli are also there… [15] The LORD God then took the man and settled him in the garden of Eden, to cultivate and care for it. [16] The LORD God gave the man this order: You are free to eat from any of the trees of the garden [17] except the tree of knowledge of good and evil. From that tree you shall not eat; when you eat from it you shall die.[j] [18] The LORD God said: It is not good for the man to be alone. I will make a helper suited to him.[k] [19] So the LORD God formed out of the ground all the wild animals and all the birds of the air, and he brought them to the man to see what he would call them; whatever the man called each living creature was then its name. [20] The man gave names to all the tame animals, all the birds of the air, and all the wild animals; but none proved to be a helper suited to the man. [21] So the LORD God cast a deep sleep on the man, and while he was asleep, he took out one of his ribs and closed up its place with flesh. [22] The LORD God then built the rib that he had taken from the man into a woman. When he brought her to the man, [23] the man said: "This one, at last, is bone of my bones and flesh of my flesh; This one shall be called 'woman,' for out of man this one has been taken." [24] That is why a man leaves his father and mother and clings to his wife, and the two of them become one body.

"Then the LORD God formed the man out of the dust of the ground and blew into his nostrils the breath of

---

[43] Rev. Fr. Robert Holet, *The First and the Finest: Orthodox Christian Stewardship as Sacred Offering* (Bloomington, IN: Author House, 2013), 3.

[44] CCC no.952 states, "A Christian is a steward of the Lord's goods."

life, and the man became a living being" (v. 7). Pope St. John Paul II states that Genesis 2:7-24 is "the oldest description and record of man's self-understanding."[45] In this passage we see some fundamental truths about the human person that concern stewardship. Adam was made of 'clay' and 'breath,' which refer to the body and soul. [46] This makes Adam's life unique from all other living things. He is the only living creature on earth alive due to God's breath dwelling in him. This is a symbolic way of expressing that Adam's life is derived from the life of God himself, indicating that he is in a personal relationship with a God.

Then we see that Adam witnessed God "plant a garden" (v. 8), fill it with trees, rivers, gold, perfume (*bdellium*) and jewels (*lapis lazuli;* vv. 12).[47] It is important to note that Adam was the only person present. In worldly terms, Adam was the wealthiest man in the world. God gave him work: to *"cultivate and care for it"* (v. 15).[48] In their document *Stewardship: A Disciple's Response* the United States Bishops elaborate,

> Genesis tells us that God placed the first human beings in a garden to practice stewardship there—"to cultivate and care for it" (Gn 2:15). The world remains a kind of garden (or workshop, as some would prefer to say) entrusted to the care of men and women for God's glory and the service of humankind.[49]

Yet, even after all of this, God observes, "It is not good that the man should be alone" (Gen 2:18).

Then God gives Adam another task: naming the animals. "So the Lord God formed out of the ground all the wild animals and all the birds of the air, and he brought them to the man to see what he would call them; whatever the man called each living creature was then its name" (v. 19). His first task was blue collar work: tilling and toiling; but this second task is white collar work: nomenclature and taxonomy. And yet, in the midst of the entire created world, amidst all his tasks, Adam has a deeper desire at play in his heart. His labors, possessions, and intelligence are not directed toward some*thing* else (he had all the "things" in the world), but toward some*one* else. He is "alone" (v.18). He is seeking a "suitable partner" (v. 18). The world, for all its stuff,

---

[45] John Paul II, *Theology of the Body,* 157.

[46] *The English-Hebrew Reverse Interlinear Old Testament New Revised Standard Version*, (Logos Bible Software 5.2a SR-7 [5.2.1.0171]), 2014, defines *nishmah* as "Breath n. — the air that is inhaled and exhaled in respiration; sometimes of the actuating principle of life." It is used 18 times in the Hebrew scripture. The more common word is *ruach* - "breeze, breath; wind; spirit; sense, mind, intellectual frame of mind. This word occurs 30 times in the Hebrew scriptures.

[47] F. Brown, S. R. Driver, & C. A. Briggs, *Enhanced Brown-Driver-Briggs Hebrew and English Lexicon* (Oxford: Clarendon Press, 1977), 995.

[48] The Hebrew word for "cultivate" (*obdah*) means to "till; to toil, work; to serve," while the word for "care" (*shamar*) means, "to keep, watch over, guard."

[49] USCCB, *Stewardship*, 9.

is inadequate for him; and what's more, he is inadequate for himself. This restless longing is an operation of his human heart causing him to search for communion.[50] Only when he found another person could he exclaim, "At last" (v. 23). Thus, we see in this passage that Adam was made for communion with both God and Eve. His wealth and work were merely a preparation for relationship.

First-fruits and Interiority: Genesis 4: 3-5

[3] *In the course of time Cain brought an offering to the LORD from the fruit of the ground,* [4] *while Abel, for his part, brought the fatty portion of the firstlings of his flock. The LORD looked with favor on Abel and his offering,* [5] *but on Cain and his offering he did not look with favor. So Cain was very angry and dejected.*

"Cain brought an offering to the LORD from the fruit of the ground, while Abel, for his part, brought the fatty portion of the firstlings of his flock" (Gen 4:3). The story of Cain and Abel sheds light on stewardship in four important points. Holet explains,

> First, the sacrificial orientation of man is present in his very nature… Secondly, the passage introduces the deeply biblical notion of offering the first fruits… Thirdly, the failure to offer worthy sacrifice is an external manifestation of sin in the heart… Finally, when a sacrificial offering is made in a righteous manner, it is acceptable to God and leads to a communion - with the one who offers and God.[51]

This ancient text shows that in the earliest history of the human person's relationship to God we bore the instinct of offering. And not just any offering, but offering our first fruits. Notice that Abel offered the best of what he had, the "fatty portion of the firstlings" (v. 4), while no such qualifier was made of Cain's offering. Holet explains, "Cain's failure is precisely a failure to offer the 'first' and the 'best.'"[52] Thus, this story teaches that offering our first fruits is an indication of holy interior intentions. A quality that is essential to the stewardship way of life.

---

[50] According to John Paul II in *Theology of the Body,* "This norm of existing as a person is demonstrated in Genesis as a characteristic of creation precisely by the meaning of these two words, 'alone' and 'help.' They point out how fundamental and constitutive the relationship and the communion of persons is for man. Communion of persons means living in a reciprocal 'for,' in a relationship of reciprocal gift. And this relationship is precisely the fulfillment of 'man's' original solitude" (*TOB*, 182).

[51] Holet, *The First and the Finest,* 6-7.

[52] Ibid., 5.

A Response of Gratitude: Genesis 14:1-20

[17] When Abram returned from his defeat of Chedorlaomer and the kings who were allied with him, the king of Sodom went out to greet him in the Valley of Shaveh (that is, the King's Valley). [18] Melchizedek, king of Salem, brought out bread and wine. He was a priest of God Most High. [19] He blessed Abram with these words: "Blessed be Abram by God Most High, the creator of heaven and earth; [20] And blessed be God Most High, who delivered your foes into your hand." Then Abram gave him a tenth of everything.

"Melchizedek, king of Salem, brought out bread and wine... He blessed Abram... Then Abram gave him a tenth of everything" (Gen 14: 18-20). This is the first instance the Bible speaks about giving a tenth. The order of events is the key to understanding this passage.[53] Abram had already won the victory. He did not *need* to give a tenth to secure success in battle. Rather, he gave a tenth *after* his victory. Stephen Clark concludes from this that Abram "probably did so as an offering out of gratitude to God for having given him victory."[54] Furthermore, the giving of Abram's tithe was in the context of the offering of bread and wine, a prefigurement of the Eucharist, to which we will return later. Abram's tithe was an act of gratitude given in a sacred context or, as Holet concludes, it was a "*response* to the awareness of the deliverance of God."[55] Thus, giving a tithe, is a grateful response; not a forced obligation.

Temple Tithe

The Old Testament concept of the tithe is the basis for one of the standards of what the Diocese of Wichita refers to as the "stewardship way of life." Clark states, "To 'tithe' means to take a tenth of something."[56] The word 'tithe' is mentioned thirty-eight times in the Old Testament.[57] Clark cites thirteen major Old Testament passages concerning the tithe.[58] Several important points are to be gleaned from these passages. First, tithing was foremost an act of worship (Deut 12:5-13).[59] Second, tithing was both an obligation and an act

---

53 Ibid., 8.

54 Stephen Clark, *Christian Tithing* (East Lansing, MI: The Sword of the Spirit, 2006), 4.

55 Holet, *The First and the Finest,* 9, italics in the original.

56 Clark, *Tithing,* 3.

57 St. Francis of Assisi Parish, *Living,* 4, 9, 12.

58 Lev. 27:30-33; Num 18:20-32; Deut 12:5-19; 14:22-29; 18:1-8; 26:12-15; 2 Chron 31:1-11; Neh 9:38; 10:28-39; 12:27-30; 12: 44-4; 13:4-14; Prov. 3:9-10; Tobit 1:6-8; Sirach 35:4-10.

59 "For a tithe was not given based on the needs of the priests, Temple, or the poor. It was given in recognition and gratitude for the blessings God had bestowed. Thus, every believer had a need to tithe to God, and it was first and foremost an act of worship, not merely a duty." Catholic Diocese of Wichita, *Tithing; An Act of Worship; An Act of Stewardship* (Wichita, KS: Catholic Diocese of Wichita), 2; Clark, *Tithing,* 8.

of gratitude.[60] Third, tithing was to be done in a "generous spirit… of joy" (Sir 35:8, 11). Fourth, withholding one's tithe was tantamount to robbing God, as the prophet Malachi says,

> You are robbing me. But you say, 'How are we robbing thee?' In your tithes and offerings. You are cursed with a curse, for you are robbing me; the whole nation. Bring the full tithes into the storehouse, that there may be food in my house; and thereby put me to the test, says the Lord of hosts, if I will not open the windows of heaven for you and pour down for you and overflowing blessing (Mal 3:8-10).

We see two other points in this passage as well: not giving one's tithe leads to a curse (v. 9) whereas giving one's tithe leads to "overflowing blessing" (v. 10). A seventh point is that Levites themselves gave a "tithe of the tithe" (Num. 18:26). Finally, it is surprising to note that there were in fact two tithes annually, and three tithes every few years, that amounted to twenty or thirty percent of income respectively (Tobit 1:6-8).[61] Thus the giving of a tenth is biblically rooted in the history of Israel.

Foundations of Stewardship in the New Testament

Bishop Gerber teaches, "stewardship…is not a mere human invention, nor a mere human message, nor, yet, a mere human witness."[62] Jesus Christ is the steward par excellence. He is the fulfillment of the Old Testament and he is the fullest revelation of the Father's plan for all mankind. To know Jesus well is to know fullness of life, of joy, and of self-sacrificial gift. Archbishop Thomas Murphy asked the question, "How do we develop among ourselves, our priests, our seminarians, and lay people a spirituality of giving that offers a biblical concept of stewardship?"[63] This can only be done by presenting a deeply contemplative and theologically sound exposition of the key biblical passages pertaining to stewardship. The New Testament passages to be covered contain essential concepts fundamental to a biblically-rooted understanding of stewardship.

Stewardship in the Parables

Most of the primary teachings on stewardship in the Gospels are found within parables. *Stewardship: A Disciple's Response* states, "Jesus sometimes describes a disciple's life in terms of stewardship" and then refers to two parables Matthew 25:14-17 and Luke 12:42-48.[64] Some consider that anywhere from sixteen to

---

[60] Clark, *Tithing*, 7.
[61] Ibid., 6.
[62] *McArdle, Grateful and Giving,Grateful and Giving,* Forward.
[63] USCCB, *Spirituality*, 1.

"nineteen of the major parables in the Bible relate directly to stewardship."[65] While it is outside the scope of this paper to discuss all such parables, we will focus on what Tracey Welliver calls "quintessential stewardship parable," the Parable of the Talents.[66]

The Parable of the Talents: Mt 25:14-30

[14] *"A man who was going on a journey called in his servants and entrusted his possessions to them.* [15] *To one he gave five talents; to another, two; to a third, one—to each according to his ability. Then he went away. Immediately* [16] *the one who received five talents went and traded with them, and made another five.* [17] *Likewise, the one who received two made another two.* [18] *But the man who received one went off and dug a hole in the ground and buried his master's money.* [19] *After a long time the master of those servants came back and settled accounts with them.* [20] *The one who had received five talents came forward bringing the additional five. He said, 'Master, you gave me five talents. See, I have made five more.'* [21] *His master said to him, 'Well done, my good and faithful servant. Since you were faithful in small matters, I will give you great responsibilities. Come, share your master's joy.'* [22] *[Then] the one who had received two talents also came forward and said, 'Master, you gave me two talents. See, I have made two more.'* [23] *His master said to him, 'Well done, my good and faithful servant. Since you were faithful in small matters, I will give you great responsibilities. Come, share your master's joy.'* [24] *Then the one who had received the one talent came forward and said, 'Master, I knew you were a demanding person, harvesting where you did not plant and gathering where you did not scatter;* [25] *so out of fear I went off and buried your talent in the ground. Here it is back.'* [26] *His master said to him in reply, 'You wicked, lazy servant! So you knew that I harvest where I did not plant and gather where I did not scatter?* [27] *Should you not then have put my money in the bank so that I could have got it back with interest on my return?* [28] *Now then! Take the talent from him and give it to the one with ten.* [29] e *For to everyone who has, more will be given and he will grow rich; but from the one who has not, even what he has will be taken away.* [30] *And throw this useless servant into the darkness outside, where there will be wailing and grinding of teeth.'*

"A man who was going on a journey called in his servants and entrusted his possessions to them. To one he gave five talents; to another, two; to a third, one - to each according to his ability" (Mt 25:14-15). Jones comments, "This parable primarily teaches that God's gifts, of nature and especially of grace, are held in stewardship and must not be allowed to lie idle...they are to be used to further his kingdom."[67] As suggested in the introduction to this paper, many persons too closely associate the term "stewardship" to "finances." At first

---

[64] Ibid., 19; Raymond E. Brown, *The Parables of the Gospels* (Glen Rock, NJ: Paulist Press, 1963), 25. See Appendix A for Raymond Brown's table of parables from *The Parables of the Gospel* with the those in bold that could be considered directly related to stewardship.

[65] McArdle, *Grateful and Giving,* 67; Gerber, *Human Love,* 13; St. Francis of Assisi Parish, *Living,* 4.

[66] Tracey Earl Welliver, *Everyday Stewardship: Reflections for the Journey* (New Berlin, WI: Liturgical Publications, 2015), 136.

[67] A. Jones, "The Gospel of Jesus Christ according to St. Matthew," in B. Orchard & E. F. Sutcliffe, eds., *A Catholic Commentary on Holy Scripture* (New York: Thomas Nelson, 1953), 897.

glance, the term "talent" used in this passage could reinforce such an association. After all, as James Gavigan

comments, "a talent was not any kind of coin but a measure of value worth about fifty kilos (one hundred and

ten pounds) of silver."[68] It was a "significant amount of wealth."[69] And yet common scriptural interpretations

consistently ascribe a much broader understanding to the term talent. For example *Stewardship: A Disciple's*

Response states, "The silver pieces of this story stand for a great deal besides money."[70] The Navarre Bible

Commentary identifies this broader meaning as "personal endowments,... natural abilities and aptitudes,...

financial resources,... spiritual gifts,... [or possibly even] the knowledge of the mysteries of the kingdom of

heaven."[71] The commentator then concludes, "Each of these interpretations represents a legitimate way to

read the parable and apply its lessons today."[72] Similarly, the Catechism lists "...physical abilities, intellectual or

moral aptitudes, the benefits derived from social commerce, and the distribution of wealth" (1936). Thus, what

is communicated by the idea of a 'talent' is not merely wealth, but that we are all endowed with a certain

variety of gifts.

The parable continues to say that he gave the talents "...to each according to his ability" (Mt 25:14-15). We

are all endowed with differing degrees of gifts, as indicated by the five talents, two talents, or one talent.[73] The

Catechism tells us, "The talents are not distributed equally," and then continues,

> These differences belong to God's plan, who wills that each receive what he needs from others, and that those endowed with particular "talents" share the benefits with those who need them. These differences encourage and often oblige persons to practice generosity, kindness, and sharing of goods (CCC, #1937).

The Bishops document on stewardship echoes this, saying that it is not that, "each has received a different

'sum'" that matters.[74] What matters is that all persons have been endowed with their own unique set of gifts.

As Vatican II states, "The Christian faithful, having different gifts (Rom. 12:6), according to each one's

---

[68] James Gavigan, Brian McCarthy, Thomas McGovern, eds., *Saint Matthew's Gospel* (New York: Four Courts Press, 2005), 161-162.

[69] Ibid.

[70] USCCB, *Stewardship*, 19.

[71] Gavigan et. al*., St. Matthew's Gospel,* 161-162.

[72] Ibid.

[73] Thomas Aquinas, *Catena Aurea: Commentary on the Four Gospels, Collected out of the Works of the Fathers: St. Matthew*, ed. J. H. Newman (Oxford: John Henry Parker, 1841), vol. 1, 853.

[74] USCCB, *Stewardship,* 20.

opportunity, ability, charisms and ministry (1 Cor. 3:10) must all cooperate in the Gospel" (Ad Gentes (AG), 28).

The parable continues: "After a long time the master of those servants came back and settled accounts with them" (v. 19). This verse reveals three key characteristics of stewardship: mutual trust, responsibility, and accountability. The master in this parable *trusted* the stewards with his property. But, also, the faithful stewards *trusted* the master to reward their ingenuity while the lazy servant did not. The master's trust included rewarding the servant's *responsibility* in carrying out the task of a steward. "Well done, my good and faithful servant… Come, share your master's joy" (v. 21). Consequently, the master expected a return on his gift. Thus he asked the lazy servant, "Should you not then have put my money in the bank so that I could have got it back with interest on my return" (v. 27)? He held each servant *accountable* according to the measure of the talents he bestowed upon them. So central is this parable to the concept of stewardship that the Bishops' definition of a steward, stated above, is almost entirely based on it. God has entrusted each of us with a differing gifts as responsible and accountable stewards.

The Widow's Mite: Luke 21:1-4

1 When he looked up he saw some wealthy people putting their offerings into the treasury 2 and he noticed a poor widow putting in two small coins. 3 He said, "I tell you truly, this poor widow put in more than all the rest; 4 for those others have all made offerings from their surplus wealth, but she, from her poverty, has offered her whole livelihood."

The story of the Widow's mite provides an example of stewardship (Luke 21:1-4) that needs little elucidation. "She, from her poverty, has offered her whole livelihood" (Lk 21:4). This passage is not so much about the coins as it is about the total surrender of one's self into God's hands. As R. Ginns observes, "She is an excellent example of that complete self-surrender which Jesus demands of his followers."[75] Holet comments,

> This encounter speaks most eloquently to the nature of sacred offerings and the importance of the *intent in the heart* of the one who offers… The widow's offering was an offering of totality… that far exceeded the notion of the first fruits offering or percentage (as in a tithe).[76]

The two copper coins here, which were the last of her sustenance, were secondary to her trust in God, from

---

[75] R. Ginns, "The Gospel of Jesus Christ according to St. Luke," in *A Catholic Commentary on Holy Scripture.* Eds. Bernard Orchard and Rev. Edmund Sutcliffe (Edinburgh: Thomas Nelson, 1958), 964.

[76] Holet, *The First and the Finest,* 28.

whom all sustenance flows. The physical giving of her coins was an outward sign of an inner trust and, as such, an explicit act of worship.

From Tithe to Total Gift

The word 'tithe' appears only eleven times in the New Testament all of which refer to the Old Testament practices already discussed. Clark observes, "In the New Testament, the practice of tithing is not spoken about very much."[77] Among the more startling practices we saw in the Old Testament was the presence of two or three tithes depending on the year. Some might find it comforting that Jesus never posited a 'tithe,' let alone a certain percent of giving. One might conclude that he intended to abolish the practice; and, in a certain sense, that idea is correct.

Jesus didn't teach a tithe, rather he taught, "If you wish to be perfect, go, sell what you have and give to the poor, and you will have treasure in heaven, and come, follow me" (Mt 19:21). Jesus does not speak of a certain percent. Rather, he speaks of total giving. The widow gave "her whole livelihood" (Lk 21:4). The rich young man was instructed to "sell what you have" (19:21). The early disciples, "had all things in common; they would sell their property and possessions and divide them among all according to each one's need" (Acts 2:44-45). And they also sold their "lands, or houses... and brought the proceeds...and laid it at the Apostles feet" (Acts 4:34-35).

So, again in a certain sense Jesus abrogated the ten, twenty, or thirty percent of the Old Testament; but he replaced it with the expectation of giving all. Clark explains,

> [Jesus] indicated rather that what the old covenant people did to follow the law should be a minimum for his disciples. They should even be more generous with their possessions than the scribes and Pharisees were (Lk 16:14 and, e.g. Lk 14: 12-14).[78]

The Diocese of Wichita summarizes this teaching in its own way,

> Jesus in fact called his followers to a standard of giving going far beyond the tithe. He called us to give up everything and follow Him, not just 10%. Hence the supreme model of giving in the New Testament was not based on a 10% tithe, but on a one hundred-percent commitment of personal resources. Jesus is the example of this 100% giving. [79]

---

[77] Clark, *Tithing*, 8.
[78] Clark, *Tithing*, 9.

Thus, Jesus proposes a new standard, or really re-proposes what was in fact the lesson we saw "in the beginning" (Gen 1:1): Everything is gift. St. Paul rhetorically asks, "What do you possess that you have not received" (1Cor 4:6-7). The answer is nothing. And St. James reminds us, "All good giving and every perfect gift is from above, coming down from the Father of lights" (1:17). Since all is gift, we must recognize that all we possess properly belongs to God. Thus we are called to give of our first fruits even as Jesus himself is the first fruits of God's own gift (1 Cor 15:20).

The Concept of Charisms in the New Testament

All people are endowed with natural gifts. Being commissioned by God to "cultivate and care" (Gen 2:15) for the earth and to "name" (Gen 2:19) creation, the human person is endowed with "dominion" (Gen 1:26, 28) over the things of the earth that, we saw, are universally destined for the good of all people. But, with outpouring of the Holy Spirit through the ministry of Christ a new dispensation has been ushered into human history. Now, united in Christ and confirmed in the Spirit, new gifts, supernatural gifts, called charisms, are bestowed upon us to carry out the work of ministry.

Charism (*charisma*, or the plural *charismata*) is variously translated as "spiritual gift," "spiritual aids," "'favor', 'gratuitous gift,' or 'benefit' (CCC, #2003)."[80] Murphy teaches they are supernatural gifts insofar as they are directly bestowed upon "each and every Christian" by the Holy Spirit and not merited as any particular reward.[81] The primary passages outlining charisms are: 1 Cor 12:7-11; 28-30, Rom 12:6-9, 1 Pe 4:8-11 and Eph 4:11-13.[82] These passages delineate twenty-two charisms: wisdom, knowledge, faith, healing, miracles, prophecy, tongues, interpretation of tongues, discernment of spirits, apostleship, teaching, assistance, administration, ministry, exhortation, giving, leadership, mercy, hospitality, service, evangelizing, and pastoring.[83]

---

[79] Clark, *Tithing*, 9.

[80] Peter S. Williamson, "Charisms," in *New Catholic Encyclopedia* (2010 supplement electronic ed.), 254.

[81] Gabriel Murphy, *Charisms and Church Renewal* (Rome: Catholic Book Agency, 1965), 49-52, 53.

[82] The Greek word is found 16 times in the New Testament, 15 times in Pauline texts and once in a Petrine text: Rom 1:11; 5:15, 16; 6:23; 11:29; 12:6; 1 Cor 1:7; 7:7; 12:4, 9, 28, 30, 31; 2 Cor 1:11; 1Tim 4:14; 2 Tim 1:6; 1 Pet 4:10.

[83] Sherry Waddell adds six more to this list: craftsmanship, music, celibacy, intercessory prayer, voluntary poverty, and writing. Sherry Weddel, *Forming Intentional Disciples: The Path to Knowing and Following Jesus* (Huntington, IN: Our Sunday Visitor: Kindle Edition, 2012), 230-232.

Most scholars agree that these lists are suggestive of the variety of gifts available, rather than exhaustive.

What are the purposes of charisms?[84] The glossary of the Catechism teaches that they "directly or indirectly benefit the Church, help a person live out the Christian life, and serve the common good in building up the Church" (CCC glossary). In other words, the gifts the Holy Spirit bestows upon a Christian a certain function within the community that aids both them and those whom they serve.

It is important to note that charisms, while supernatural, do not eliminate a person's own natural ability.[85] Rather, as Bishop Martinez says, charisms can inform a person's natural talents giving them a fluidity and effectiveness "of a truly divine character."[86] Still, at other times, charisms can come to a person as an independent gift that had little precedent in a person's natural abilities. We will revisit this concept of charisms later.

Promised Gift, Sacred Worship: 2 Corinthians 9:5-15

5 So I thought it necessary to encourage the brothers to go on ahead to you and arrange in advance for your promised gift, so that in this way it might be ready as a bountiful gift and not as an exaction. 6 Consider this: whoever sows sparingly will also reap sparingly, and whoever sows bountifully will also reap bountifully. 7 Each must do as already determined, without sadness or compulsion, for God loves a cheerful giver. 8 Moreover, God is able to make every grace abundant for you, so that in all things, always having all you need, you may have an abundance for every good work. 9 As it is written: "He scatters abroad, he gives to the poor; his righteousness endures forever." 10 The one who supplies seed to the sower and bread for food will supply and multiply your seed and increase the harvest of your righteousness. 11 You are being enriched in every way for all generosity, which through us produces thanksgiving to God, 12 for the administration of this public service is not only supplying the needs of the holy ones but is also overflowing in many acts of thanksgiving to God. 13 Through the evidence of this service, you are glorifying God for your obedient confession of the gospel of Christ and the generosity of your contribution to them and to all others, 14 while in prayer on your behalf they long for you, because of the surpassing grace of God upon you. 15 Thanks be to God for his indescribable gift!

One of the most common phrases used in stewardship formation is, "God cannot be outdone in

---

[84] *Lumen Gentium* 12 delineates eight purposes of charisms: they "sanctify and lead the people of God,... are "special graces" given to individuals, ...make individuals "fit and ready" for their "tasks and offices," ...are aimed at the "renewal and building up of the Church," ...are to be received with "thanksgiving and consolation," ...can either be "outstanding" or "more simple," ...do not guarantee the "the fruits of apostolic labor" ...and, finally, are judged to be genuine by "appointed leaders in the Church."

[85] "In their actual exercise, however, charisms and natural abilities are frequently found together. The Holy Spirit builds upon, and perfects, a person's natural capacities." Cardinal Avery Dulles, "The Charism of the New Evangelizer," in *Retrieving Charisms for the Twenty-First Century* (Collegeville, MN: The Liturgical Press, 1999), 36.

[86] Luis M. Martinez, *The Sanctifier* (Paterson, NJ: St. Anthony Guild Press, 1957), 123.

generosity." This phrase finds root in 2 Cor 9:5-11.[87] In seeking to inspire the communities' generosity Paul

assures them of God's overwhelming abundance which, in turn, inspires trust within their act of generosity. He

says, "God is able to make every grace abundant for you, so that in all things, always having all you need, you

may have an abundance for every good work" (2 Cor 9:8). Paul's exhortation in these passages echoes that of

the Gospel, "Without cost you have received, without cost you are to give (Mt 10:8)."

Of significance for the concept of stewardship is St. Paul's "promised gift" (v. 5). In fact, the Greek word,

eulogia, which can be translated as "gift," appears four times in verses 5 and 6, "So I thought it necessary

to…arrange in advance for your promised gift (*eulogia*), so that it might be ready as a bountiful gift (*eulogia*) and

not as an exaction… whoever sows bountifully (*eulogia)* will reap bountifully (*eulogia*)." In the first instance of

the word gift Paul refers to it as a "promised gift" (*proepenggelmenen eulogian*). This gift was "promised" per

St. Paul's instructions to the Corinthians in his first visit: "On the first day of the week, each of you is to put

something aside… so that contributions need not be made when I come… to carry your gift to Jerusalem" (1 Cor

16:1-2). In this sense, a correlation can be made between Paul's "promised gift" and the modern act of

pledging. Furthermore, this pledge is to be collected "as a bountiful gift not as an exaction (*pleonexia*)" (v. 5).

St. Paul wants to protect the joy of giving and to avoid "sadness or compulsion (v. 7)," so he concludes, "God

loves a cheerful giver" (v. 7).

Four times St. Paul assures the Corinthians of God's blessings:

1. He who sows bountifully, will reap bountifully (v. 6).
2. God is able to make every grace abundant for you, so that in all things, always having all you need, you may have an abundance for every good work (v. 8).
3. God will multiply your seed (v. 10).
4. You are being enriched in every way for all generosity (v. 11).

Like a battering ram on a castle door, St. Paul is repeatedly assuring the Corinthians that God will protect their

generosity from causing them lack.

Solidarity is the climatic concept of this passage. Verse 12 and 13 develops this concept of solidarity in

three Greek terms: *diakonia, leitourgia, and koinonia.*

---

[87] See also Rom 15:25-27; 1 Cor 16:1-2; 2 Cor 8-9; Gal 2:10.

27

For the administration (*diakonia*) of this public service (*leitourgia*) is not only supplying for the needs of the holy ones but is also overflowing in many acts of thanksgiving to God. Through the evidence of this service (*koinonia*) you are glorifying God (2 Cor 9:12-13).

All three of these words carry a double meaning. *Diakonia* can mean simultaneously "service" as well as "arrangement for support or contribution."[88] *Leitourgia* adds a religious and sacrificial overtone to the collection. John MacEvilly observes that it nuances the pledge with a sense of "sacred service" but also "denotes worship activity."[89] Stegman agrees, "Here Paul understands the collection as tantamount to an act of worship."[90] And St. Paul concludes that this *diakonia* and *leitourgia* "provide evidence...of...the generosity of your service (*koinonia*)" (v. 13). Again, as in the first two terms, *koinonia* can refer to both "communion" as well as a "willing contribution." Stegman explains,

> The word for 'contribution' here is *koinōnia*, which means, fundamentally, 'fellowship' or 'communion.' Paul thereby indicates that God is glorified when we commit ourselves to promoting the *koinōnia*, or communion, of the larger Church.[91]

Thus, all three terms emphasize the interconnectedness between the financial contribution and the solidarity within a community. So to summarize: one who administers (*diakonia)* the sacred service (*leitourgia)* brings about communion (*koinonia)* as an act of sacred worship.[92] Ultimately, the participation in the collection is an imitation of Jesus' own self-emptying.

Self-Emptying, Self-Donation: Philippians 2:5-8

[5] *Have among yourselves the same attitude that is also yours in Christ Jesus,* [6] *Who, though he was in the form of God, did not regard equality with God something to be grasped.* [7] *Rather, he emptied himself, taking the form of a slave, coming in human likeness; and found human in appearance,* [8] *he humbled himself, becoming obedient to death, even death on a cross.*

---

[88] James Swanson, *Dictionary of Biblical Languages with Semantic Domains: Greek (New Testament)* (Oak Harbor, WA: Logos Research Systems, Inc, 1997), electronic ed. "*diakonia.*"

[89] John MacEvilly, *An Exposition of the Epistles of St. Paul and of the Catholic Epistles* (New York: Benziger Brothers, 1898), vol. 1, 335–336.; Stegman, *Second Corinthians,* 217, respectively.

[90] Stegman, *Second Corinthians,* 217–218.

[91] Ibid., 218.

[92] Clark succinctly explains, "Tithing is an act of homage... that expresses a relationship of honor and submission to the Lord and the order he appoints for people to come near to him. Tithing is not just a practical arrangement to meet certain needs, but it is an act of worship to the Lord and acknowledgment of his provision and direction for his people" (*Tithing,* 11).

We have seen how Jesus didn't simply abrogate the tithe but returned his disciples to "the beginning" where all is gift (Gen 1:1). He does not seek a certain "percent" from us but he wants us to recognize that all we possess is gift, including our very lives. In Phil 2:5-8 St. Paul holds up Jesus himself as supreme model of sacrificial self-gift. He says, "Have among yourselves the same attitude that is also yours in Christ Jesus" (v. 5). The Greek verb meaning "have this attitude" (*phroneō*) used here means that, "Christians are to not only imitate but also assimilate into themselves Jesus' way of thinking."[93] This means that they are to regard "everyone else as more important than themselves and to put everyone else's interests ahead of their own."[94]

Jesus is the supreme example of this, "who though he was in the form of God, did not regard equality with God something to be grasped" (v. 6). In other words, Jesus did not lord his exalted status as Son of God over people. Rather, "he emptied himself, taking the form of a slave" (vs. 7). The verb 'to empty' here is *kenoō* meaning "to cause to lose power, be emptied, empty oneself, divest oneself of position."[95] Elsewhere St. Paul captured this idea when he said, "Though He was rich, yet for your sakes He became poor, that through His poverty you might become rich" (2 Cor. 8:9). Jesus used his "equality with God" in humble service for all people. As the Gospel says, Jesus came to serve, not to be served (Mt 20:28).

Furthermore, his self-emptying was accomplished through a total gift of his self, a total self-donation, by "becoming obedient to death" (v. 8). This gift of self was a total abasement, "...even death on a cross" (v. 8). He "became a curse for us" (Gal. 3:13) so that we who incurred the curse of original sin might be set free by the wealth of his holiness. So we are to imitate him in his self-emptying and his self-donation. The only true tithe, the only true sacred offering, is not our possessions, but our very selves, or as St. Paul says, "I want not what is yours, but you" (2 Cor. 12:14).

Stewardship: A Disciple's Response comments, "In Jesus' teaching and life self-emptying is fundamental. Now, it might seem that self-emptying has little to do with stewardship, but in Jesus' case that is not so."[96]

---

[93] Dennis Hamm, *Philippians, Colossians, Philemon*, eds. Peter S. Williamson and Mary Healy (Grand Rapids, MI: Baker Academic, 2013), 98.

[94] Ibid, 95.

[95] Swanson, *Dictionary,* electronic ed., "*keno*."

[96] USCCB, *Stewardship,* 19.

Jesus' self-emptying and self-donation engender gratitude, elicits a response, and encourages imitation. Wichita adds, "The more we reflect upon Jesus' total donation of self to us, despite how often we have turned away from Him, the more grateful we become."[97] This gratitude then elicits a response as St. Francis of Assisi parish's document on stewardship *Living Life as God Intended It* teaches, "Parishioners who fully appreciate the magnitude of Jesus' daily gift of Himself will full appreciate the debt we owe in return."[98] This response then encourages us to imitate him. *Stewardship: A Disciple's Response* teaches, "Here also Jesus is the model. Even though his perfect self-emptying is unique, it is within the power of disciples, and a duty, that they be generous stewards."[99] And the document concludes that this response is expressed concretely, "...giving freely of their time, talent, and treasure."[100] Thus as Jesus gave of himself completely so to stewards are called to give completely of themselves as well.

The Four Pillars of Stewardship: 1 Peter 4:7-11

[7] The end of all things is at hand. Therefore, be serious and sober for prayers. [8] Above all, let your love for one another be intense, because love covers a multitude of sins. [9] Be hospitable to one another without complaining. [10] As each one has received a gift, use it to serve one another as good stewards of God's varied grace. [11] Whoever preaches, let it be with the words of God; whoever serves, let it be with the strength that God supplies, so that in all things God may be glorified through Jesus Christ, to whom belong glory and dominion forever and ever. Amen.

St. Peter states, "As each one has received a gift, use it to serve one another as good stewards of God's varied grace (1 Pet 4:10)." This is the most quoted verse in stewardship literature and McGread considered this the vision statement of stewardship.[101] Yet what is not always seen is that this passage read in context (1 Pet 4:7-11) contains references to the four pillars of stewardship proposed by the Diocese of Wichita – (1) prayer, (2) hospitality, (3) formation and (4) service – characterized by *agape*.

It begins with (1) prayer and (2) hospitality: "Therefore, be serious and sober for prayers. Above all, let your love for one another be intense... Be hospitable to one another without complaining" (1 Pet 4:7-9). These

---

[97] Catholic Diocese of Wichita, *Characteristics of a Christian Steward* (Wichita, KS: Catholic Diocese of Wichita, 1999), 27.

[98] St. Francis of Assisi Parish, *Living*, 4.

[99] USCCB, *Stewardship,* 31-32.

[100] Ibid.

[101] St. Francis of Assisi Parish, *Living*, 27.

first three verses describe Peter's expectation of Christian conduct: prayer, *agape*, and hospitality.[102] These

three practices can be understood in terms of love: prayer, as the exercise of the love of God, and *agape* and

hospitality as the exercise of the love of neighbor.

Peter begins, "Be serious and sober for prayers (v. 7)." To be 'serious and sober,' according to D.C.

Arichea means "…to keep one's head… to keep your senses awake."[103] Prayer is the way in which one keeps

their eyes fixed on the "end of all things" (v. 7). The Catechism glossary defines prayer as "the elevation of mind

and heart to God in praise of his glory". Taking these two points together we see that through prayer one

discerns God's will to apply it in our present actions of stewardship.

Our prayerful attentiveness comes to fruition in *agape*, or self-sacrificial love. As Paul's phrase, "above

all" (v. 8), indicates, *agape* is the motivation for Christian conduct. It is also the motivation of the stewardship

way of life according to the Diocese of Wichita's definition of stewardship. But this is not just any love, but

agape love: self-sacrificial love that is revealed in Jesus' self-emptying and self-donation.

This *agape* is exercised through hospitality as St. Peter says, "Be hospitable to one another" (v. 9).

MacEvilly observes that the biblical concept of hospitality included three spheres: welcome of missionaries, care

for strangers, and openness for 'house-churches'.[104] Hospitality is an exercise of the *koinonia* discussed earlier.

Now we come to the hallmark stewardship passage. "As each on has received a gift, use it to serve one

another as good stewards of God's varied grace" (1 Pet 4:10). St. Peter uses the term steward - *oikonomos.*

Stewardship: A Disciple's Response explains,

> An *oikonomos* or steward is one to whom the owner of a household turns over responsibility for caring
> for the property, managing affairs, making resources yield as much as possible, and sharing the
> resources with others. The position involves trust and accountability.[105]

As Keating explains, "The word "steward" (*oikonomos*) builds on the root word "house" (*oikos*),"[106] thus

---

[102] Daniel Keating, *First and Second Peter, Jude,* eds. Peter S. Williamson and Mary Healy (Grand Rapids, MI: Baker Academic, 2011), 102.

[103] D. C. Arichea & E. A. Nida, *A Handbook on the First Letter from Peter* (New York: United Bible Societies, 1980), 138.

[104] MacEvilly, *An Exposition,* Vol. 2, 355–356.

[105] USCCB, *Stewardship,* 19.

[106] Keating, *First and Second Peter, Jude,* 104.

confirming the Bishops' comment.

Notice that St. Peter directly connects the terms "gifts" (*charisma*), discussed earlier, and "stewards" for us. Keating states, "All of us are called to be stewards of the spiritual gifts we have been given for the service of our brothers and sisters."[107] As charisms, these gifts do not simply refer to natural talents, but also, spiritual gifts (1 Cor 12:31). Clark refers to these as "ministry gifts" or "the way God equips someone to do a service."[108] We will return to this point later.

The rest of this passage completes the last two pillars of stewardship: (3) formation and (4) service. "Whoever preaches (*laleō*), let it be with the words of God; whoever renders service (*diakonia*), let it be done with the strength God supplies" (v. 11). These are two modes of proclamation: "speaking" and "serving" or word and action.[109] In terms of stewardship preaching refers to the pillar of formation and service to the pillar of the same name.

MacEvilly explains that the term "to preach" encompasses all the variations of the charisms of speech, "by which is meant...the exercise in the Church the gift of *wisdom*, or *knowledge*, or *prophecy, doctrine, exhortation, interpretation*."[110] J.D. Barry adds that "The word translated *preach* may refer to the gift of prophecy or to any type of speaking about God and the truth of the gospel."[111] Thus, "to preach" refers to formation.[112]

One is to also exercise gifts of service. Here, again, as in 1 Cor 9:13, the word used is *diakonia*. Arichea

---

[107] Ibid.

[108] Stephen Clark, *Charismatic Spirituality: The Work of the Holy Spirit in Scripture and Practice* (Cincinnatti, OH: St. Anthony Messenger Press, 2004), 90.

[109] Keating, *First and Second Peter, Jude*, 104.

[110] MacEvilly, *An Exposition*, vol. 2, 356.

[111] J. D. Barry, et. al., *Faithlife Study Bible* (Bellingham, WA: Lexham Press, 2012, 2016), 1 Pet 4:11.

[112] A question can be asked if the term "preaches (*laleō*)" can adequately refer to the pillar of formation. When one looks at the occurrences of the term (*laleō*), meaning to "**speak**, talk; ... tell," one gets the sense that it can (*Swanson*, electronic ed. *"laleō"*). This term is used in three primary ways: to proclaim the Gospel, to speak sound doctrine, and to use upright speech (Arichea, 142). It appears a total of 50 times in the New Testament. Of these, the lion's share has to do with evangelical preaching and doctrinal teaching. Keating's comments help support this claim, "But given the general context ("as each has received a gift"), we should apply this to all Christians, whenever they are speaking of God and serving his people. Peter is not telling his readers to act as prophets uttering oracles, but simply as people who communicate what God has to say. Since Scripture is a rich source of the sayings of God and Christ, no Christian is unsupplied with 'the words of God.' If we are immersed in God's Word, then we are in a position to speak 'the words of God' in whatever situation we find ourselves in." (*First and Second Peter, Jude,* 105).

explains that this word refers to, "any kind of service or ministry, which in the early church included feeding the hungry, caring for the sick, helping the poor, and welcoming strangers."[113] Whereas we saw that "to preach" included all the charisms of speech, "to serve" includes all the charisms of service such as healing, help, administration, contributing, giving aid, and acts of mercy.[114]

Trinitarian Foundation of Stewardship

The culminating passage of our scriptural study is Trinitarian: "Go, therefore, and make disciples of all nations, baptizing them in the name of the Father, and of the Son, and of the holy Spirit" (Mt 28:19). This passage points to both the mission of the Church, which we will discuss later, but also the Trinitarian foundation of the life of stewardship. Concerning this Bishop Gerber teaches,

> Stewardship is rooted in the relationship of the three Divine Persons. From all eternity the divine relationship of Father, Son, and Holy Spirit are altogether mutual, reciprocal, and interdependent. From the very first God intended Adam and Eve and their descendants to be drawn fully into the communion which the three divine persons enjoy. The central teaching of the Greek Fathers is that the Christian life is not simply to make us better people, ethically upright, but to make us divine, to conform us to a participation in the life of the Trinity.[115]

Stewardship imitates the Trinity under the aspect of mutual reciprocity. Gerber goes on to say, "Jesus is always present drawing us more nearly, more dearly, more clearly into the mutual reciprocity and interdependent relationships which the Father, the Son, and the Holy Spirit enjoy without beginning or end."[116] The Trinity invites us into this mutual reciprocity by imitating the self-emptying and self-donation of, not just Jesus, but of all three Persons. The Father emptied himself to us in his Son, as St. Paul says, "He who did not spare his own Son but handed him over for us all, how will he not also give us everything else along with him" (Rom 8:32)? Jesus then emptied himself to us as John testified, "He loved his own in the world and he loved them to the end" (Jn 13:1). Then the Spirit was showered upon us as St. Paul says, "the love of God has been poured out into our hearts through the holy Spirit that has been given to us" (Rom 5:5). In addition, Vatican II explains that the whole apostolate is based on the life of the Trinity,

---

[113] Arichea, *A Handbook,* 142.
[114] 1 Cor 12:28 and Rom 12:6, 8.
[115] Gerber, *Human Love,* 5.
[116] McArdle, *Grateful and Giving,* Foreword.

The lay person should learn especially how to perform the mission of Christ and the Church by basing his life on belief in the divine mystery of creation and redemption and by being sensitive to the movement of the Holy Spirit who gives life to the people of God and who urges all to love God the Father as well as the world and men in Him. This formation should be deemed the basis and condition for every successful apostolate (AA, 30).

Jesus also prays, "may all be one, as you, Father, are in me and I in you, that they also may be in us" (Jn 17:21). Indeed, our communion (*koinonia*) with the Trinity is Jesus' explicit desire. We realize this communion in mutual reciprocity through the Holy Spirit. *Living Life as God Intended It* teaches, "Our faith is about relationships. Through Christ we learn of the relationship between God the Father, God the Son, and God the Holy Spirit... At the heart of any relationship lie give and take."[117] And Gerber expounds, "Prime among the many gifts that come with being created in God's image and likeness is the capacity 'to give' and 'to receive.'"[118] This mutual reciprocity is part of God's plan and the root of the stewardship way of life.

There is a close connection between God's plan and the life of stewardship. God's plan for salvation is called the "economy of salvation." The Catechism indicates that the Greek word for "economy" is *oikonomia.* It defines this word as, "God's revelation and communication of himself to the world in time for the sake of the salvation of all humanity" (CCC, Glossary). The catechism includes in this definition that it means "management of a household" or "stewardship" (CCC, Glossary). Notice the closeness of these two words in Greek: economy (*oiknonomia*) and steward (*oikonomos*), spoken of earlier. Now, as we have already seen, a steward is a "manager of a household," an "administrator," or "one who has authority and responsibility for something."[119] When one places two terms side by side, one sees that stewardship is the unique participation of a disciple in God's plan of salvation. A steward (*oiknomos*) is one who has a part to play in the plan of God (*oikonomia*). So *Stewardship: A Disciple's Response* teaches, "God wishes human beings to be his collaborators in the work of creation, redemption, and sanctification; and such collaboration involves stewardship in its most profound sense."[120]

In the final analysis the most fitting image of stewardship is the Father, the Son, and the Holy Spirit, who

---

[117] St. Francis of Assisi Parish, *Living,* 5.
[118] McArdle, *Grateful and Giving,* Foreword.
[119] Swanson, *Dictionary,* electronic ed., "*oikononmos.*"
[120] USCCB, *Stewardship,* 25.

are a Communion of Persons. The interior life of the Trinity consists in self-gift and beckons us to that same self-gift. This was the lesson Adam learned in the beginning. All of his 'stuff' didn't satisfy the restless longing of his heart. He was made for a communion of persons with God and neighbor. Jesus is the ultimate example of the total gift of self. He emptied himself for us so that we might know how to empty ourselves for others. The stewardship way of life is a realization of communion in imitation of the Trinity through the example of Jesus Christ. As Bishop Gerber concludes, "Through our time, talent, and treasure we are brought into communion with our brothers and sisters… we are drawn into the divine relationships that are all together mutual, reciprocal, and interdependent."[121]

---

[121] Gerber, *Human Love*, 11.

Chapter 3 - The Magisterial Foundations of Stewardship

Children are fascinated with echoes. Whether in a valley or in a round-topped foyer, children have fun yelling out and hearing the reverberation of sound. Just as echoes reverberate sound so the Church echoes the truths of scripture throughout her history. But unlike normal echoes that lose strength and clarity, the articulation of truth gains clarity and strength as they are handed on over time. So too the truths of stewardship found in Scripture find further clarity as they are articulated by the Church's magisterium over time. Let us now turn to the magisterial foundations of stewardship.

The Apostolate

The documents of Vatican II never use the word stewardship and use the word steward only four times (*Lumen Gentium* (LG), 13, 21, 26; *Apostolicam Actuostatem* (AA), 3). But the documents do teach much about the stewardship way of life in their teaching about the apostolate. Vatican II states, "Christian vocation by its very nature is also a vocation to the apostolate" (AA, 2). As such, apostolic action is proper to both clergy and laity. The *Code of Canon Law* (CIC) echoes, "Since they participate in the mission of the Church, all the Christian faithful have the right to promote or sustain apostolic action even by their own undertakings" (no. 216). Understanding stewardship in terms of the apostolate rather than in terms of raising funds helps to correct many mistaken understandings of this way of life. The Decree on the Laity defines the apostolate,

> The Church was founded for the purpose of spreading the kingdom of Christ throughout the earth for the glory of God the Father, to enable all men to share in His saving redemption, and that through them the whole world might enter into a relationship with Christ. All activity of the Mystical Body directed to the attainment of this goal is called the apostolate, which the Church carries on in various ways through all her members (AA, 2).

The term 'stewardship,' as it is understood in Wichita, bears this accent of meaning. Stewardship is the apostolate in practice for both clergy and laity.

Code of Canon Law succinctly applies the apostolate to the laity,

> Since, like all the Christian faithful, lay persons are designated by God for the apostolate through baptism and confirmation, they are bound by the general obligation and possess the right as individuals, or joined in associations, to work so that the divine message of salvation is made known and accepted by all persons everywhere in the world. This obligation is even more compelling in those circumstances

in which only through them can people hear the gospel and know Christ (225).

Lumen Gentium defines the laity as "all the faithful except those in holy orders and those in the state of religious life specially approved by the Church" (33). The lay apostolate is essential to both the life of the Church and the individual.[122] As Vatican II goes on to say, the laity "have their own share in the mission of the whole people of God" (AA, 2); so much so that, "...the member who fails to make his proper contribution to the development of the Church must be said to be useful neither to the Church nor to himself" (AA, 2).

The laity are called to exercise their role in the apostolate both "in the Church and in the world" (LG, 33) in both "the spiritual and temporal orders" (AA, 5). Too often Christian men and women dissociate their life of faith from their life in society. But this cannot be the case for the lay apostolate, nor for a true steward. As the document on the Church in the Modern World warns,

> Let there be no false opposition between professional and social activities on the one part, and religious life on the other... The split between the faith which many profess and their daily lives deserves to be counted among the more serious errors of our age (Gaudium et Spes, 43).

Within the Church, Vatican II teaches, the laity are able to function in "more immediate cooperation with the hierarchy" and "pastors should confidently entrust the laity with duties in service of the Church" (AG, 21, *Presbyterorum Ordinis* (PO) 9). Pope St. Paul VI teaches, "This can be done through the exercise of different kinds of ministries according to the grace and charisms which the Lord has been pleased to bestow on them" (*Evangelii Nuntiandi* (EN), 73). This cooperation furthermore should be done by "allowing them freedom and room for action" (PO, 9).

This freedom to act should not be undervalued. Recall that the stewardship way of life in Wichita was promoted by strong lay leadership fostered by various lay movements. Freedom for lay activity is one on the four indispensable ingredients of the stewardship way of life in a parish.

An ancient document in the Church says, "Christians must be to the world what the soul is to the body."[123] This beautiful image portrays the rich ministry that the laity bring into every sphere of their influence. As the

---

[122] Vatican II states, "The Church can never be without it" (AA, 1). And again, "No part of the structure of a living body is merely passive but has a share in the functions as well as life of the body" (AA, 2).

[123] From a letter to Diognetus, *The Christians in the World* (prepared by the Spiritual Theology Department of the Pontifical University of the Holy Cross) (Nn. 5-6; Funk, 397-401), accessed August 8, 2017. http://www.vatican.va/spirit/documents/spirit_20010522_diogneto_en.html.

Code of Canon Law states,

> According to each one's own condition, [the laity] are also bound by a particular duty to imbue and perfect the order of temporal affairs with the spirit of the gospel and thus to give witness to Christ, especially in carrying out these same affairs and in exercising secular functions (216.2).

This is precisely where the stewardship of the laity differs from the stewardship of the clergy. The primary concern of the clergy is life within the Church, whereas the primary concern of the laity is the message of the Gospel in secular society "like leaven" (AA, 2; LG, 31; AG, 15). As *Lumen Gentium* clarifies, "The laity are called in a special way to make the Church present and operative in those places and circumstances where only through them can it become the salt of the earth" (33). The presence of the laity in the world is a salve that heals the culture even as it "permeates and transforms it" (AG 21).

Scott Hahn, in his book *Evangelizing Catholics,* distinguishes the various 'fields' of the lay apostolate as the Christian family, friendship, the neighborhood, the workplace, the parish, and other specialized fields.[124] Of these various fields special mention should be made of the "domestic church," the family, which *Lumen Gentium* calls the "excellent school of the lay apostolate" (11, 35). Gerber directly states, "Stewardship is not worth the dignity of its word without honoring and defending marriage and family life."[125] And Wichita continues, "It is in the family, then, where Christ's self-donating love is first taught and learned."[126] Vatican II adds, "the whole family in its common life, then, should be a sort of apprenticeship for the apostolate" (AA, 30). It is here, Vatican II continues, where even young people learn how "their natural qualities, fit them for this activity" (AA 12). And still further children "also have their own apostolic work to do" (AA, 13). In Wichita, youth and children are invited into stewardship by being asked to fill out their own time and talent forms as well as being encouraged to use youth envelopes for financial giving.[127]

The apostolate is not only concerned with the family or the parish but extends "to interparochial, interdiocesan, national, and international fields" (AA, 10). Thus there is a truly universal duty within the practice

---

[124] Scott Hahn, *Evangelizing Catholics: A Mission Manual for the New Evangelization* (Huntington, IN: Our Sunday Visitor, 2014), 98-117.

[125] Gerber, *Human Love*, 21.

[126] CDOWK, *Characteristics of a Christian Steward,* 5.

[127] St. Francis of Assisi Parish, *2017 Stewardship Time and Talent Grades 9-12 in 2017-2018* (Wichita, KS: Catholic Diocese of Wichita, 2017); St. Francis of Assisi Parish, 2017 *Stewardship Time and Talent Grades 6-8 in 2017-2018* (Wichita, KS: Catholic Diocese of Wichita, 2017).

of stewardship as well.[128] This duty is carried out in the Diocese of Wichita in three ways. First, the diocese and its parishes support missions through *United Catholic Stewardship*, which we will explain later. The parishes directly support missions through their own efforts such as youth or adult mission trips or ministries devoted to supporting missions. Finally, some individuals and even whole families offer their stewardship as true missionaries following the summons of *Ad Gentes* to go to "forsaken areas of their own diocese or of other dioceses" (20).

Discipleship and Stewardship

Discipleship precedes stewardship. The apostolate, and consequently stewardship, is contingent upon discipleship. As Wichita's definition explains stewardship is a "response of a Christian Disciple." Like a top losing centrifugal force, if, in the life of an individual or parish, anything is placed before discipleship the whole system falls out of balance.

Discipleship is a "living union with Christ" (AA, 4). *Stewardship: A Disciple's Response* teaches, "Mature disciples make a conscious, firm decision, carried out in action, to be followers of Jesus Christ no matter the cost to themselves."[129] The Bishops continue "…discipleship requires the surrender of ourselves through grace and choice to Jesus Christ."[130] This 'cost' is central to the life of discipleship: "Whoever wishes to come after me must deny himself, take up his cross, and follow me. For whoever wishes to save his life will lose it" (Mt 16:24-25). The soul of stewardship is imitating Jesus in his own self-emptying. For this reason every day is to be lived with close personal familiarity with Jesus.[131] As McGread teaches, "This is how pastors are able to reach parishioners. Emphasize Christ!"[132] And so Bishop John J. McRaith stated, "Once one becomes a Disciple of Jesus Christ, stewardship is not an option."[133]

What then is the difference between stewardship and discipleship? Some persons have posited that

---

[128] This is clearly outlined in the Diocese of Wichita, "This sharing of gifts is characterized primarily through the home, extending to the parish, to the entire diocese, to the wider community and to the universal church." Catholic Diocese of Wichita, *The Relationship Between Stewardship and Development in the Catholic Diocese of Wichita* (Wichita, KS: Catholic Diocese of Wichita, 2014), 2; CDOWK, *Tithing*, 1.

[129] USCCB, *Stewardship*, 5.

[130] Ibid, 1.

[131] Ibid, 14.

[132] McArdle, *Grateful and Giving*, 72.

[133] USCCB, *Stewardship*, 1; 14.

they are the same thing.[134] But the Bishops' document on stewardship clarifies, "stewardship does not totally

encompass the concept of discipleship [but it] 'sheds a certain light' on discipleship."[135] And continues,

"Stewardship is an expression of discipleship, with the power to change how we understand and live out our

lives."[136]

To draw an analogy, stewardship is to discipleship what family love is to spousal love. Spouses love one

another with a love different than parents love their children or children love their parents. Just as spousal love

is different from familial love, so too discipleship is different from stewardship. Disciples are devoted to Jesus

Christ like one spouse is devoted to another: intimate, individual, and a total self-gift. Yet, by being devoted to

the same Jesus Christ disciples thereby become brothers and sisters in Christ and share a familial love. And just

like in a household every member has a share in its responsibilities; so too, stewardship is the share of

responsibilities each disciple bears for the functioning of the "household of God" (1 Tim 3:15). Pope Francis

made this point in a Vatican interview. Cindy Wooten, writing for Catholic News Service, reports,

> The Vatican II dogmatic constitution on the church, "*Lumen Gentium*," described the style of
> relationships within the church as "familial," the pope said. Viewing the church as a family emphasizes
> shared responsibility, mutual support and joint action while, at the same time, recognizing the special
> role of guidance belonging to the church's pastors, he said.[137]

Stewardship: A Disciple's Response echoes this teaching, "Disciples of Jesus Christ are stewards of the Church

because stewardship is the personal responsibility of each one of the baptized."[138] Wichita sees this

responsibility as an aspect of familial love, "Like a blood family, the parish family stands ready and eager to

collectively wrap their arms around their brothers and sisters when they suffer in trial and/or celebrate special

events in their lives."[139] So stewardship and discipleship are two sides of the same reality but they are exercised

---

[134] Bishop Jackels posited this: "What is discipleship? A shared life of self-gift in service. What is Stewardship? A shared life of self-gift in service" (John Lanzrath, *The Spirituality of Stewardship,* (Wichita, KS: Catholic Diocese of Wichita, 2010), Lesson 1, DVD.

[135] USCCB, *Stewardship*, 19.

[136] Ibid., 5.

[137] Wooten, Cindy, *"Pope Says Laypeople Share Responsibility for Church,"* *Catholic News Service*, August 23, 2012, accessed July 25, 2017, http://www.catholicnews.com/services/englishnews/2012/pope-says-laypeople-share-responsibility-for-church.cfm.

[138] USCCB, *Stewardship*, 2.

[139] Catholic Diocese of Wichita, *The Pillars of Parish Stewardship* (Wichita, KS: Catholic Diocese of Wichita, 2004), 22.

with two distinct loves. Remaining indispensable to one another, discipleship determines one's identity in Christ while stewardship describes one's mission to fellow disciples. Discipleship is an exercise of faith in the living God. Stewardship is the work that exemplifies that faith (James 2:18). As Gerber says, "There is an insistence on the need for faith, but there is also the demand that faith without good works is dead."[140]

Stewardship and Holiness

Stewardship is intimately associated to a life of holiness. Gerber explains, "The 'timing' for today's stewardship came in the wake of the Second Vatican's Council's universal call to holiness."[141] Indeed, the goal of stewardship is to sanctify oneself and one's neighbor. As *Lumen Gentium* clearly taught, "All are called to sanctity and have received an equal privilege of faith through the justice of God" (32). The holiness to which the family of Christ must strive is both a personal holiness and a holiness proper to body of Christ. As *Lumen Gentium* goes on to say, "The faithful... must assist each other to live holier lives even in their daily occupations" (36). Stewardship trains in holiness by turning parishes into schools of prayer and increasing the quality of the Sunday liturgy (CCC, #2689; Novo Millennio Ineunte, 33). Thus, in living a life of stewardship, one is also set on the path of holiness.

Stewardship and Evangelization

Just as stewardship and discipleship are related, so too, stewardship and evangelization are similarly related. *Stewardship: A Disciple's Response* teaches, "the practice of authentic Christian stewardship inevitably leads to evangelization."[142] Stewardship depends immediately on its fidelity to discipleship and commitment to evangelization. They are, so to speak, the front and back end of stewardship. Just as a long train can have engines pulling from the front and pushing from the back, so stewardship will lose momentum if it is not situated between the two engines of discipleship and evangelization. The Bishops' document then concludes,

> In various ways, then, stewardship of the Church leads people to share in the work of evangelization or proclaiming the Good News, in the work of catechesis or transmitting and strengthening the faith, and in works of justice and mercy on behalf of persons in need.[143]

---

[140] Gerber, *Human Love,* 11.
[141] *McArdle, Grateful and Giving,* Foreword.
[142] USCCB, *Stewardship,* 9.
[143] Ibid., 32.

What is Evangelization?

What, then, is evangelization? Evangelization is the proclamation of the good news of salvation in Jesus Christ with the goal of leading people to discipleship through faith and conversion.[144] It seeks to convert not only the person but also, as Pope Paul VI says, "the collective consciences of people, the activities in which they engage, and the lives and concrete milieu which are theirs" (EN 18). The great commission of Mt 28:19-20 commands us to make disciples, baptize them into the life of the Trinity, and to teach all that Jesus said and did. Evangelization can be directed to the mission "ad gentes" (meaning "to the nations"), to pastoral care within the Church, and the re-evangelization of fallen away Catholics or Catholics who have never been fully catechized (EN 15, 33). These last two properly refer to the work of what is called the "new evangelization."

Evangelization is the obligation of "every disciple of Christ according to his state" (LG, 17). This obligation is achieved through the personal witness of the Christian faith "by deeds," such as works of mercy and charity, and the announcement of Christ "by words," such as preaching and teaching (AA 6, 19). It must be expressed with an urgency that never loses confidence in the permanent power of the word and must be proclaimed with *parrhesia*, or boldness (*Redemptoris Missio* (RM), 1; EN, 42; RM, 45). It seeks the transformation of culture beginning with the heart of individuals (EN 18).[145] Finally, it effects true "changes in patterns of Christian living" which restores "all things in Christ" (EN, 44; Eph 1:10). In the end, no one is fully evangelized until they evangelize others (EN 24; RM 2). Evangelization is achieved through the proclamation of the *kerygma*.

What is the Kerygma?

What, then, is the kerygma? The kerygma is the basic proclamation of the Gospel. Essentially Jesus Himself is the kerygma. He is the Good News we are called to proclaim. His very name means "God saves." The kerygma is not an "optional contribution" for the Church but is the "first and fundamental way of serving" (EN 5;

---

[144] United States Conference of Catholic Bishops, *Go and Make Disciples: A National Plan and Strategy for Catholic Evangelization in the United States* (Washington, D.C.: United States Conference of Catholic Bishops, 2002), Kindle location 48-49.

[145] ibid.

RM 20). When it is preached with *parrhesia* (boldness) it contains an explosive character with a unique power to awaken faith in those who listen. This is because it contains the Word, who is Jesus Christ, and the Life of the Spirit unto the glory of God for the salvation of souls.

John 3:16 is the most succinct scriptural summary of the kerygma, "For God so loved the world that he gave his only Son, so that everyone who believes in him might not perish but might have eternal life." Contained within this passage are the five constitutive elements of the kerygma. These five elements can be remembered by the acronym G.R.A.C.E., as St. Paul says, we are "saved by grace" (Eph 2:8). G.R.A.C.E. stands for: **G**od's love for the world, **r**epentance from sin, the **a**dvent of Jesus Christ, **c**onfessing his name, and the gift of **e**ternal life. Let us briefly elaborate on each phrase.

G – **God's love** is the 'leading step' when proclaiming the Gospel. This love is personal, unconditional and eternal. It is a love that earnestly desires us to be in full communion with the God who is perfect Communion.

R - But we must **repent** in order for this communion to be received (Mt 3:2). Sin has separated us from God and has left the human race in a situation of enmity with him. "Personified evil" induced our first parents to sin by promising a false freedom that only led to slavery (GS, 2). If sin goes unrepentant then we will eternally perish.

A – But God did not abandon us. "God… sent his only Son" (Jn 3:16) to free us from this horrible fate. Through the **advent** of Jesus, God came to seek and save the lost, forgive us of our sins, and bestow on us the grace of divine adoption.

C - Now by **confessing** faith in Jesus we personally commit to following him as his disciple. Cleansed by Baptism, made 'one flesh' with Jesus through the Eucharist, and anointed by the Holy Spirit in Confirmation we are gifted and inebriated. Our lives are visibly changed. We live differently as we share the message mercy, repentance, and salvation (Mt 28:19).

E – Because of this Jesus has opened the real possibility of **eternal life** to us. We are saved by the gratuitous act of Jesus Christ who overthrows the effect of sin, routes the devil and establishes the eternal

Kingdom of God. We receive this eternal life by believing and following Jesus.

Stewardship and Mission

Stewardship, then, is a participation in the mission of evangelization. This is our mission: to preach the kerygma, thereby inviting people to become disciples of Jesus Christ, and caring for fellow believers as stewards of God's gifts. James Mallon makes the jolting assertion that, "It's not so much that the Church of Christ has a mission, as that the mission of Jesus Christ has a Church."[146] In other words, the people of God have been called together to proclaim the one faith revealed in Jesus Christ.[147] As *Stewardship: A Disciple's Response* states, "Being sent on a mission is a consequence of being a disciple."[148] And the *Code of Canon Law* goes on to explain,

> Since the whole Church is by its nature missionary and the work of evangelization must be held as a fundamental duty of the people of God, all the Christian faithful, conscious of their responsibility, are to assume their part in missionary work (CIC, no.781).

To be missionary does only not mean to engage is some fantastical overseas activity. Rather, to be missionary is to proclaim the kerygma in every 'field' of apostolic activity spoken of earlier. An essential characteristic of an ideal parish is to be missionary. Peter Williamson posits, "A parish cannot be a closed or inward looking community, but rather, missionary, outward-looking, welcoming, and inclusive in all that it does."[149] Pope Francis states, "I dream of a "missionary option," that is, a missionary impulse capable of transforming everything… parishes must become more mission-oriented" (*Evangelii Gaudium*, 27). Pope Francis challenges parishes to become missionary.

> The parish … can assume quite different contours depending on the openness and missionary creativity of the pastor and the community. … if it proves capable of self-renewal and constant adaptivity… it can be a community of communities… and a center of constant missionary outreach (*Evangelii Gaudium*, 28).

He continues, "Mere administration can no longer be enough… the parish must be "permanently in a state of mission" (EG, 22). And he further states, "Missionary outreach is paradigmatic for all the Church's activity… we

---

[146] Fr. James Mallon, *Divine Renovation: From a Maintenance to a Missional Parish* (New London, CT: Twenty Third Publications, 2014), 17.

[147] The Greek word for church, *"eccleisa,"* is literally translated "called out."

[148] USCCB, *Stewardship*, 14.

[149] Peter Williamson, *Vision of Ideal Parish in Light of the Paradigm of the Apostolic Church* (Ann Arbor, MI: unpublished paper, 2016), 2.

need to move from a pastoral ministry of mere conservation to a decidedly missionary pastoral ministry" (EG, 6). Or, as the popular phrase goes, parishes need to move from maintenance to mission.[150]

Stewardship is fundamentally an exercise of this missionary impulse. The pope teaches, "All of us are called to take part in this new missionary "going forth." … to obey Jesus' call to go forth from our own comfort zone in order to reach all the "peripheries" (EG, 22). No longer can we think that this is the job of a priest or a sister. Missionary work is everyone's job. He concludes "All the members of the People of God are missionary disciples… and calls for a personal involvement from each of the baptized" (EG, 120). As such, stewardship must be subordinated to discipleship and discipleship be missionary in its practice. A sense of mission is one of stewardship's three primary motivators. We will soon see the next two primary motivators.

The Church echoes with the truth of scripture expounded by the magisterium over time. This echoing is itself an act of catechesis that hands on the deposit of faith from one generation to the next. Stewardship finds clarity within the documents of the magisterium. Stewardship is an aspect of the apostolate that derives its motivation from the mission of discipleship. Called to holiness the disciple shares his faith and life by preaching the kerygma through evangelization. Let us now turn our attention to the interior meaning of the stewardship way of life as a spirituality of giving.

---

[150] Robert Rivers, *From Maintenance to Mission*: *Evangelization and the Revitalization of the Parish* (New York, NY: Paulist Press, 2005), Kindle Location 310.

Chapter 4 - The Stewardship Way of Life

Stewardship is the *grateful response of a Christian disciple who recognizes and receives God's gifts and shares these gifts in love of God and neighbor*. This is not just any way of life but, as McGread says, a "radical way of life."[151]   McGread elaborates: "It is not a program. It is a way of life. A program has a beginning and an end; but the stewardship way of life goes on forever."[152] Fr. Ken Schuckman, a priest of the Diocese of Wichita, succinctly captured this idea,

> Stewardship is a way of life. It is not something we turn on and off. It is like breathing. Once it becomes part of our life it happens very naturally. Those who have experienced the true joy and peace of stewardship do not see stewardship as a burden but rather the only true way to live as Disciples of Christ.[153]

McGread further states, "a pastor needs to understand, stewardship as a spiritual awakening within his own parish, his own community, and his own life."[154] The core spirituality of stewardship is founded upon a theology of giftedness. Indeed, *Stewardship: A Disciple's Response* calls stewardship a "spirituality of giving."[155] Everything we have, everything we are, is a sheer gift of God's love. Our very existence is gift. We did not create ourselves. We did not give ourselves life or the ability to experience all the beautiful things God has made. Everything that exists has been made without us; and yet we rejoice in it all as if it were ours. Gerber states, "The spirituality of stewardship is the grateful acknowledgment that all is gift."[156] McGread echoes, "It all hinges on recognizing that everything we have are all gifts from God – our time, and our talents, and our treasure, even our very lives."[157] Clements refers to this as, "the principal key that unlocks the stewardship message," and Wichita calls it "the fundamental point of stewardship."[158] Bishop Carl Kemme, current Bishop of Wichita,

---

[151] McGread, Jan. 26, 2012, Blog.

[152] McGread, *Foundation,* Video.

[153] Rev. Kenneth Schuckman, "Stewardship Renewal Letter" (presented by letter to the parishioners of St. Mary's, Newton, KS, November 1, 1997).

This 'breathing' reminds us of man's first breath 'in the beginning.' God blew his breath into Adam, "and so Adam became a living being" (Gen 2:7). Our discipleship began by breathing in the grace of Jesus Christ that came to us through no merit of our own but rather through faith. In the words of St. Augustine, "You breathed your fragrance on me; I drew in breath and now I pant for you" (F. J. Sheed (trans.), *The Confessions of St. Augustine* (New York, NY: Sheed & Ward, 1943), Chpt. XXVII). Stewardship is the disciple's intentional sharing of God's breath in a free response to new life.

[154] *McArdle, Grateful and Giving,* 70.

[155] USCCB, *Stewardship,* 1.

[156] Most Rev. Eugene J. Gerber, E-mail interview, July 19, 2017.

[157] *McArdle, Grateful and Giving,* 15.

[158] Clements, *Time, Talent and Treasure,* Kindle Locations 252-253.; CDOWK, *Characteristics,* 35.

summarizes this main point,

> There is nothing we have; nothing; that is not a gift. Everything we are and everything we have is founded in the loving generosity of the Creator. When we know this, not just in our minds but in the depths of our hearts, then life takes on a whole new meaning. Then we have a whole different perspective about our time or our talents or our treasure, our bodies, our minds, hearts – everything that we are and everything that we have – takes on a completely different perspective.[159]

Stewardship is a grateful response to God's abundant gifts. In order to come to a deeper understanding of the spirituality of stewardship let us discuss the key term and phrase of Wichita's definition, namely, gratitude, response, Christian Disciple, recognizes and receives, God's Gifts, shares, and finally, love of God and neighbor. We will then briefly look at the characteristics of a steward as well as some blessings and obstacles of the stewardship way of life.

A Steward is Grateful

Gratitude is the necessary response to gift. As the story of the ten lepers concludes, "One of them, realizing he had been healed, returned glorifying God in a loud voice; and he fell at the feet of Jesus and thanked him." (Lk 17:16). Fr. John Lanzrath, former director of the Office of Stewardship in the Diocese of Wichita, states, "The heart of a Christian steward is gratitude."[160] McGread also states, "As Christian stewards, it is of utmost importance that we see God as the great gift-giver and thank Him for all He has given us. In fact, that is where our lives as Christian stewards ought to begin, because without Him, we would have nothing."[161] And again, "This is the basis for the stewardship way of life: a thanksgiving. How important it is that we thank Him for what he does for us."[162]

The primary mentality of a Christian steward is an attitude of gratitude. Gratitude is like harvesting a field: one can only pick the grain one notices, but if the grain is never noticed then it can never be harvested. Gratitude, as Abram exemplified, is recognizing God's blessings so that we can honor him for what he has done on our behalf. Gerber states, "A grateful heart silences a complaining voice."[163] Common Preface IV in the Mass

---

[159] CDOWK, *Stewarding*, 4.

[160] Lanzrath, *Spirituality*, Lesson 1, DVD.

[161] McGread, April 21, 2011. Blog.

[162] Ibid., Dec. 5, 2013.

[163] Lanzrath, *Spirituality*, Lesson II, DVD.

states, "You have no need of our praise, yet our desire to thank you is itself your gift." [164] Gratitude is its own gift and the second of three true motivators for the stewardship way of life. Gerber states that this is, "...not because we expect a return, as if interest on a loan, but simply to express a heartfelt thanks to God for the gift of life and what we enjoy, whether little or much."[165] A steward prioritizes gratitude before any thought of return.

Stewardship is a Faith Response

The third and most important motivator for embracing the stewardship way of life is faith. Faith in God leads to gratitude for his blessings. A sense of gratitude leads to a sense of mission by which one shares the faith that is gratitude's source. So faith, gratitude, and mission – these are the three primary motivators of the stewardship way of life. The Bishops, in *Stewardship: A Disciple's Response*, teach that stewardship is a "faith response."[166] Just as the widow had faith in God's care for her and just as St. Paul wanted to bolster the faith of the Corinthians in God's abundance, this response of faith arises from the confidence of a disciple who knows, with certainty, that God cannot be outdone in generosity (2 Lk 21:1-5; 2 Cor 9:8).[167] Gerber explains, "To live in the will of God is to realize that we need nothing other, that we crave nothing more, that we can let go of everything else."[168] Kemme also reminds us, "Stewardship is not just about one or another aspect of our faith lives; it is about all of it."[169] Thus faith is exercised as total confidence in God the Father who is totally trustworthy (Lk 11:11-14).[170] As *Living Life as God Intended It* states, "pastors and lay leaders must exhibit absolute trust and confidence in stewardship as a way of life."[171]

This faith response is a consequence of a personal invitation. McGread teaches, "This way of life is by

---

[164] Catholic Church, *The Roman Missal: Renewed by Decree of the Most Holy Second Ecumenical Council of the Vatican, Promulgated by Authority of Pope Paul VI and Revised at the Direction of Pope John Paul II (Third Typical Edition)* (Washington D.C.: United States Conference of Catholic Bishops, 2011), 616.

[165] Gerber, email interview.

[166] USCCB, *Stewardship,* 50.

[167] Gerber, *Human Love,* 1; St. Francis of Assisi Parish, *Living,* 3.

[168] Gerber, *Human Love, 3.*

[169] CDOWK, *Stewarding,* Intro.

[170] This truth about stewardship carries an evaluative weight in considering practical applications to parish stewardship activities. Every approach a parish adopts must respect stewardship as a faith response and avoid coercive or manipulative practices.

[171] St. Francis of Assisi Parish, *Living,* 17.

invitation only." If a person is not personally invited then he may wonder if he is personally wanted. The Bishops invite young adults to stewardship, "This is a call to young adults everywhere to renew the face of the earth. This is a call to listen to the voice of the Spirit speaking of gratitude and responsibility. This is an invitation to Catholic stewardship."[172] Indeed, the Bishops' purpose in writing *Stewardship, A Disciple's Response*, was, "to invite, and challenge, all members of the Catholic community to accept their baptismal responsibility to place their gifts, their resources, their selves at God's service in and through the Church."[173]

A Steward is a Christian Disciple

The call to stewardship is in consequence of one's call to discipleship. A disciple is "one who responds to Christ's call."[174] This call is rooted in the sacraments of initiation. In calling teenagers to a life of stewardship the Bishops explain,

> In Baptism you were called to the common priesthood of Jesus Christ—showing Christ's presence in the world; you were called to be a prophet—speaking the truth courageously; and you were called to the kingly role of serving others lovingly. In Confirmation or Chrismation, you receive the power to live this call by the gift of the Holy Spirit. The Eucharist sustains you and gives you the strength to respond to this call even when you don't feel like responding![175]

Our life of stewardship is intimately linked to our identity in our vocation.[176] Gerber explains, "Stewardship helps us to discover our vocation and live it, identify our personal dignity, and respect it, recognize God's prompting and embrace it."[177] God calls us each, personally, "by name" (Jn 10:3). So, again, the Bishops encourage young people,

> Everyone has a calling, which is another way of saying that your walk with God is personal. When you hear the call to gratitude and responsibility—in your friendships and family, in your work, wherever you go—then taking the next step to answer that call is where Catholic stewardship may be clearly seen.[178]

The *Code of Canon Law* succinctly states this call, "All the Christian faithful must direct their efforts to lead a holy life and to promote the growth of the Church and its continual sanctification, according to their own condition"

---

[172] United States Conference of Catholic Bishops, *Stewardship and Young Adults* (Washington D.C.: USCCB, 2003), 1.

[173] USCCB, *Stewardship,* 50.

[174] Ibid, 9.

[175] United States Conference of Catholic Bishops, *Stewardship and Teenagers* (Washington D.C.: USCCB, 2007), 2.

[176] Gerber, *Human Love,* 3.

[177] *McArdle, Grateful and Giving,* foreword.

[178] USCCB, *Young Adults,* 2.

(CIC, no.210).

Stewardship, like discipleship, requires conversion. Through conversion disciples learn to make a sincere gift of themselves and their goods to others. *Stewardship: A Disciple's Response* states, "In the lives of disciples, however, something else must come before the practice of stewardship. They need a flash of insight—a certain way of seeing—by which they view the world and their relationship to it in a fresh, new light."[179] Indeed, one may even come to discipleship by practicing stewardship. Gerber explains,

> Stewardship is a decision of the will not a feeling, although good feelings often follow. We can't wait for our attitudes regarding stewardship to change our behavior. By changing our behavior our attitudes will change to match the Gospel way of life.[180]

So discipleship and stewardship mutually lead to one another. As McGread expounds,

> Stewardship begins with a conversion of heart. The true steward makes a commitment to the Lord – not merely to the parish. He gives His life to God because He wants to follow Him, and everything else – his time, his talent, and his treasure – follows suit. … That being said, however, it is important to recognize that some of your parishioners may come to conversion through participation in parish ministries.[181]

A Steward both Recognizes and Receives

You cannot be a steward of gifts you do not recognize you possess. We have already seen that gratitude itself is a form of recognition. We must develop the ability to notice all the good things God has bestowed upon us… in good times and in bad. As Lanzrath states, "The steward's eye begins to see and recognize all that is good comes from God."[182] As athletes train their reflexes, so stewards train their ability to recognize God's gifts in every circumstance. *Stewardship: A Disciple's Response* teaches, "The stewardship of disciples is not reducible only to one task or another. It involves embracing, cultivating, enjoying, sharing—and sometimes also giving up—the goods of human life."[183] We would be completely destitute were it not for the love of God who has given us everything. As Jesus says, "Without me you can do nothing," and as James says, "All good giving and every perfect gift is from above" (Jn 15:5; James 1:17). So Gerber concludes, "Christian stewards realize that the

---

[179] USCCB, *Stewardship*, 39.

[180] Most Rev. Eugene J. Gerber, *"A Bishop's Journey to Stewardship"* (Paper presented at the annual International Catholic Stewardship Conference, Toronto, Canada, October 28th, 2002), 8-9.

[181] McGread, July 14, 2011. Blog.

[182] Lanzrath, *Spirituality,* Lesson 3.

[183] USCCB, *Stewardship*, 28.

ownership of all we have, including time, belongs elsewhere; ours is only the privilege of use."[184]

The Bishops' document on stewardship goes on to say that a steward is "one who receives God's gifts gratefully, cherishes and tends them."[185]A common saying in the Church is, "You cannot give what you do not have (*nemo dat non quod habet*)." It is not enough to recognize our gifts but we must also receive them. As St. Augustine is purported to say, "The God who created you without you, will not save you without you." We must always be cooperators with the gifts God has bestowed upon us. *Lumen Gentium* encourages, "Every person should walk unhesitatingly according to his own personal gifts and duties in the path of a living faith which arouses hope and works through charity" (41). This unhesitating reception then begins a cycle of giftedness. Lanzrath explains, "God gives the gift of life and love. I must receive that gift of life and love. I must accept that gift of life and love. I must allow the gift of life and love to transform me. I must share the gift of God's life and love."[186] Gift given... gift received... gift accepted... gift transformed... gift shared – this is the cycle of giftedness.

A Steward possesses God's Gifts

To what do "God's gifts" refer? When people think of the gifts of stewardship they frequently think of time, talent, and treasure, but conceive of these in earthly terms. The phrase is often de-spiritualized. Time is often seen as "another event to schedule," talent is understood as "skills" or mere "volunteerism," and treasure is seen as "money." It should be clearly stated that the earthly aspect is necessary. St. Thomas taught that, "grace does not destroy nature, but perfects it."[187] And St. Paul's "natural man" is still the root of the "spiritual man" (1 Cor 2:14). Clark emphasizes that we must not "overlook the importance of using natural skill and human effort for ministries and services."[188] So efforts at stewardship renewal that focus on natural talents that lead to volunteerism or on material needs are not inimical to stewardship per se. Yet, it is necessary to understand "God's gifts" more richly as spiritual gifts, or charisms.

---

[184] Gerber, *Human Love*, 6.

[185] USCCB, *Stewardship*, 9.

[186] Lanzrath, *Spirituality*, Lesson 3.

[187] Thomas Aquinas, *Summa theologica* (Fathers of the English Dominican Province, Trans.) (London: Burns Oates & Washbourne), I q.1 a.8 ad 2.

[188] Clark, *Charismatic Spirituality*, 100.

Recall our discussion of charisms earlier. St. Paul explained that their purpose is to "equip the saints, for the work of ministry, for the building up of the body of Christ" (Eph 4:12). Cantalamessa teaches, "The purpose of charisms, then, is *diakonia*, or service or ministry" and they are "for the enrichment… the vitality and variety of the Church."[189] Clark makes a distinction between the spiritual nature of a charism and a mere skill. "[Charisms] are called gifts or graces (favors), because they are not something we can earn or acquire by our own efforts, like the skill attested by a medical degree, but are the result of the Holy Spirit working in us "as he wills."[190] As such, he goes on to say, they are "the gifts and graces of the Spirit as equipping us or 'programming' us, making us 'spiritual receptors.'"[191] Thus "God's gifts" must refer to spiritual gifts as much, if not more, than simply natural gifts.

But there is an even deeper meaning to the spiritual understanding of the term "gifts" in relation to stewardship. It is this: the various gifts, or charisms, are actually a kaleidoscope reality of the one Gift of the Spirit himself. Just as white light is made up of the various colors of the spectrum, so too, individual charisms are various hues of the one Holy Spirit (1 Cor 12:11). Cardinal Joseph Ratzinger teaches, "The Holy Spirit always is in his essence the gift of God, God as the self-donating, so as the self-distributing, as gift."[192] And Clark adds, "the gifts of the Spirit, especially the charismatic gifts or spiritual gifts, do not function apart from the giver Himself."[193] Thus, when the definition of stewardship refers to "God's gifts" these gifts ultimately refer to the Spirit himself who dwells within us as in a temple (1 Cor 6:19).

Now the Spirit is "the Lord and Giver of Life" as our Creed tells us. Thus, in bearing the Gift of the Spirit within us, we are also bearing the source of Life within us. Lanzrath comments, "God enters into the life of the human so that the human can enter into the life of the divine."[194] Ratzinger takes us another step further, "God communicates himself in the Holy Spirit as love."[195] Thus the gift of God we possess is both Life and Love.

---

[189] Raniero Cantalamessa, *Intoxicating Power of the Spirit* (Collegeville, MN: Liturgical Press, 1994), 66.
[190] Clark, *Charismatic Spirituality*, 79.
[191] Clark, *Charismatic Spirituality*, 83.
[192] Ibid., 331.
[193] Clark, *Charismatic Spirituality*, 81.
[194] Lanzrath, *Spirituality*, Lesson 1.
[195] Joseph Ratzinger, "The Holy Spirit as Communio: Concerning the Relationship of Pneumatology and Spirituality in Augustine," *Communio* 25 (1998), 328.

Connecting these together, "God's gifts" can be seen as natural gifts, spiritual gifts, *The* Gift Himself (the Holy Spirit), who then dwells in us as Life and Love.

But one last step must be taken to come full circle back to natural gifts. The gift of God is the Holy Spirit who unites us in one body of Christ, or one communion (*koinonia*). Recall from earlier that *koinonia* has a dual meaning of "communion" as well as a "willing contribution." A full understanding of the term *koinonia* is the cotter pin of this "full-circle." Thomas Smail explains,

> The root meaning of *koinonia* is a having in common, the sharing of common life. It can be used to describe an intimate spiritual union of persons,… [or] the sharing of money and possessions, which was one of the first results of the pouring out of the Spirit at Pentecost (Acts 2:44).[196]

Thus, the term "gifts" in the definition of stewardship needs to be understood as spiritual charisms building upon natural gifts rooted in the indwelling Holy Spirit who himself is Life and Love and who unites the community in his Person through concrete action expressed by sharing time, talent, and treasure thereby fulfilling Jesus' desire, "may all be one, as you, Father, are in me and I in you" (Jn 17:21). We will revisit this point later.

A Steward Shares

Now, all of this is ours to share: our natural gifts, our spiritual gifts, our *koinonia*; and finally, *the* Gift of Life and Love who is the Holy Spirit. Stewardship is the active branch of our discipleship. Stewardship is to discipleship what exercise is to a gym membership. Just because one is a member of a gym does not mean that one is exercising. In the same way, just because one is a disciple does not mean one is a steward. St. Francis of Assisi, in collaborating with its parishioners, articulates in its *Parish Family Agreement*, "Discipleship calls us to more than membership; it calls us to an active stewardship… Stewardship is an act of belonging and involvement. It is an act of recognizing God's providence to us and our obligation to manage it wisely."[197] *Stewardship: A Disciple's Response* teaches, "Sharing is not an option for Catholics who understand what membership in the Church involves… a comprehensive view of stewardship [is] a vision of sharing, generous, accountable way of life, rooted in Christian discipleship."[198] For this reason the Bishops refer to stewardship, not

---

[196] Thomas Smail, *The Giving Gift: The Holy Spirit in Person* (London: Hodder & Stoughton, 1988), 182.
[197] St. Francis of Assisi Parish, *Parish Family Agreement* (Wichita, KS: Catholic Diocese of Wichita, 2016), 1.

only as a spirituality of giving, but also as a "spirituality of sharing."[199] The Bishops exhort teenagers to this life

of sharing,

> Everything you have to share is from God, and it is all meant for sharing. Being a disciple means sharing without counting the cost. Being a disciple means sharing even when we least feel like it, when we least can afford to do it, and when the person in need of our gift is the last person we wish to serve.[200]

There is, in fact, a double dignity that is upheld by this sharing. The person sharing recognizes he or she has

something to offer, thereby speaking to a personal dignity. The one receiving is recognized and worthy of one's

time and talent, thereby speaking of his or her personal dignity. Thus a double dignity is implicit in every act of

stewardship.

The fact is this: everyone has something to offer. Gerber says, "As disciples, living stewardship as a way

of life, we offer our entire selves, including our personalities, natural talents, temporary and permanent

charisms, education, life experiences and background to God to be used for his purposes."[201] So *Stewardship: A*

Disciple's Response concludes, "the basic underlying value or conviction [is] that self-giving is good for the

spiritual health and vitality of the individual, family, or community.[202]

The human person, created in the image of God who gives, is created with a need to give. The God who

shares creation with us asks us to share creation, including our very life, with others. We have a need to give.

Living Life as God Intended It states, "Stewardship is primarily based on the person's need to give in gratitude,

rather than on the church's need to receive. Stewardship is not about fund raising or volunteer recruitment, it is

about spirituality, education, and conversion."[203] Furthermore, this need to give is to be done without

expectation of return. Jesus teaches "If you lend money to those from whom you expect repayment, what

credit [is] that to you? Even sinners lend to sinners, and get back the same amount" (Lk 6:34).

We are also called to give out of our need, not out of our surplus. Remember the story of the widow's

mite. She gave out of her need, not her surplus. Consider too the story of the widow of Zarepheth. Elijah asked

---

[198] USCCB, *Stewardship*, 7.
[199] Ibid., 3.
[200] USCCB, *Teenagers*, 2.
[201] Gerber, *Human Love*, 11.
[202] USCCB, *Stewardship*, 64.
[203] St. Francis of Assisi Parish, *Living*, 16.

her for a biscuit and a cup of water. She replied, "As the LORD, your God, lives,… there is only a handful of flour in my jar and a little oil in my jug. Just now I was… [going] to prepare something for myself and my son; when we have eaten it, we shall die" (1 Kings 17:2). Yet, she trusted the prophet, gave out of her need, and she and her son lived with blessings. Thus, to give out of our need, not out of our surplus, is a call we each must heed.

A Steward Loves God and Neighbor

The wellspring of stewardship is this: "God is Love" (1 Jn 4:8).[204] We have already discussed several aspects of this love. The love in which stewardship is exercised is *agape*, or self-sacrificial love. Such love imitates the self-emptying, self-donating, love of Jesus who proved "his love for us in that while we were still sinners Christ died for us" (Jn 13:1). Furthermore, God's love "has been poured into our hearts through the holy Spirit that has been given to us" who now dwells in us as in a temple (Rom 5:5; 1 Cor 3:16). The love of God is the leading step of Gospel message, the *kerygma*. And this love it is expressed in prayer and hospitality for, "Whoever loves God must also love his brother" (1 Jn 4:21). As Vatican II reminds us, "Every exercise of the apostolate should be motivated by charity" (AA, 8).

"In this is love; not that we have loved God, but that he loved us" (1 Jn 4:10). Our response to this love is twofold. First we dwell in love, for "whoever remains in love remains in God and God in him" (1 Jn 4:16). Second, we share that love. "Beloved, if God so loved us, we also must love one another" (1 Jn 4:11). This love is expressed through concrete action, "If someone who has worldly means sees a brother in need and refuses him compassion, how can the love of God remain in him" (1 Jn 3:17)? So Vatican II teaches, "The laity should vivify their life with charity and express it as best they can through their works" (AA, 16). So, as Lanzrath says, "stewardship is the response of the disciple to God's unconditional love for us."[205]

Characteristics of a Christian Steward

A disciple who lives the spirituality of giving is an icon of Christ. The steward, as a disciple, bears the characteristics of Christ and witnesses him. Wichita teaches "a faithful steward is characterized by a life of

---

[204] Lanzrath, *Spirituality*, Lesson 2.
[205] CDOWK, *Pillars*, 4.

virtue" and highlights ten such virtues.[206] Here we will limit our comments to six, humility, patience, generosity, simplicity, mercy and perseverance. The other four, prayer, trust, responsibility, gratitude are discussed elsewhere.

Humility is truth about oneself under three aspects. First, without God "you can do nothing" (Jn 5:5). A steward is ever aware of his radical dependence upon God.[207] Second, a steward recognizes the truth that he is gifted and called to share those gifts in love.   Finally, a steward recognizes he does not possess all gifts. Rather, he must rely on others' gifts. There is no place for radical individualism in the Christian dispensation.

Patience is a companion to long-suffering, a fruit of the Holy Spirit. Patience is an imitation of Christ's self-emptying. Don McArdle observes, "This way of life is far from an easy one."[208] Stewardship is not for the timid, nor the weak. Knowing "God is trustworthy" does not mean we won't be stretched to the limits of our ability or trust (Jn 3:33; 1 Cor 10:13). Wichita teaches, "Patience is remaining at peace with God's will, confident that he always provides what is best for us."[209]

A steward is generous. Jesus says, "the measure you measure with will be measured back to you" (Lk 6:38). An ancient letter attributed to Barnabas teaches,

> Share with your neighbor whatever you have, and do not say of anything, this is mine. If you both share an imperishable treasure, how much more must you share what is perishable… Do not hold out your hand for what you can get, only to withdraw it when it comes to giving…Never hesitate to give, and when you do give, never grumble: then you will know the one who will repay you.[210]

A steward lives a life of simplicity. *Stewardship: A Disciple's Response* says, "Stewardship requires that many people adopt simpler lifestyles."[211] Wichita echoes this, "Simplicity challenges us to examine what we need versus what we want."[212] So Vatican II beckons us to remember, "Man is more precious for what he is than for what he has" (GS, 35). Simplicity frees one from materialism and encourages generosity.

A steward is merciful. Wichita teaches, "Mercy is the spark that fans the embers of stewardship into a

---

[206] CDOWK, *Characteristics of a Christian Steward,* 1.
[207] CDOWK, *Pillars,* 18.
[208] *McArdle, Grateful and Giving,* 69.
[209] CDOWK, *Characteristics of a Christian Steward,* 20.
[210] From a letter attributed to Barnabas, Office of Readings, Tuesday 19th week in Ordinary Time.
[211] USCCB, *Stewardship,* 26.
[212] CDOWK, *Characteristics of a Christian Steward,* 34.

fire of compassionate service... Mercy compels the already responsible steward into accepting even greater responsibility for the welfare of others."[213] So the Church holds up the Spiritual and Corporal Works of Mercy as models for stewards to follow. Mercy is shown in generous service and sincere forgiveness.

Finally, a steward needs perseverance as *Stewardship: A Disciple's Response* cautions, "Stewardship is not easy."[214] And Vatican II warns, "the laity have their work cut out for them in the life and activity of the Church" (AA, 10).

Stewardship is a way of life; as such, it is life-long as Wichita teaches,

> Because stewardship is a way of life and not a short-term endeavor, the Christian steward will need perseverance to continue on through the difficult times. For indeed, those who embrace a stewardship way of life will experience trials that call for perseverance.

The Personal Blessings of the Stewardship Way of Life

We have seen that the authentic motivators for living the stewardship way of life are faith, gratitude, and mission. And yet, because stewardship is "living life as God intended it," it bears true blessings.[215] As Gerber states, "you can't keep the rewards out of practicing stewardship any more than you can keep happiness out of virtuous living."[216] Just as the Apostles asked Jesus, "What will there be for us" (Mt 19:27), so the Bishops' teach that stewards "reasonably wonder what reward they will receive. This is not selfishness but an expression of Christian hope."[217]

> The personal blessings of stewardship are many. Bishop Gerber enumerates,

> Stewardship... leads to solidarity with the poor and the experience of one's own poverty of spirit. Stewardship gives the person living it a profound respect for life, appreciation of nature, a respect for the gift of others, and a sense of human interdependence and solidarity.[218]

And the Bishops bolster young adults saying,

> The rewards include: making a difference in people's lives; becoming an active member of a fulfilling Catholic community; discovering talents inside you, waiting to be used; letting go of your worries and setting realistic goals in both your spiritual and secular life; experiencing the amazing increase in God's presence that comes with a partnership with the Lord.[219]

---

[213] Ibid. 39.
[214] USCCB, *Stewardship*, 48.
[215] St. Francis of Assisi Parish, *Living*, title.
[216] CDOWK, *Tithing*, 16.
[217] USCCB, *Stewardship*, 20.
[218] Gerber, *Human Love*, 18.
[219] USCCB, *Young Adults*, 2.

McGread maintained that one of the greatest blessings of stewardship is that it provides standards for life.[220] Where there are no standards there can be no excellence. Standards encourage striving. Finally, and most importantly, the greatest personal benefit is "an intimate relationship with Jesus," a deeper communion with God, and participation in the life and love of the Holy Spirit.[221]

Personal Obstacles to the Stewardship Way of Life

Living the stewardship way of life can be like running an obstacle course: one must anticipate the obstacles in order to run it successfully. There are many personal obstacles to living the stewardship way of life. *Stewardship: A Disciple's Response* highlights several,

> This is a culture in which destructive "isms" - materialism, relativism, hedonism, individualism, consumerism - exercise seductive, powerful influences. There is a strong tendency to privatize faith, to push it to the margins of society, confining it to people's hearts or, at best, their homes... excluding it from the marketplace.[222]

Like an odor one gets used to, or a slow poisoning, these "ism's," being so much a part of our culture, can often affect us even without our awareness.

Other obstacles stem from a lack of formation, trust, and priority.[223] Stewardship is not an intuitive way of life. Therefore it takes sincere effort to learn its meaning, adopt its habits, and inculcate its values. A lack of historical knowledge leads to a lack of appreciation. Further, it must never be forgotten that this is a faith-based life. It demands trust that casts out fear as God says, "Do not fear... you are mine" (Is 43:11). Also, if one does not prioritize the 'spirituality of giving' in one's life then other concerns and anxieties will take its place. Luxury, inordinate wants, selfish ambition all erode the soil upon which stewardship stands.

Not least among the obstacles are complacency and fatigue. Gerber elucidates these obstacles as, "lack of fervor, fatigue, disenchantment, compromise, lack of interest, and lack of joy and hope. But worst of all, indifferentism."[224] In contrast *Stewardship: A Disciple's Response* reminds us that "Jesus' call is urgent."[225] But

---

[220] McArdle, *Grateful and Giving,* 14.
[221] Gerber, email interview.
[222] USCCB, *Stewardship*, 5.
[223] CDOWK, *History*, 4.
[224] Gerber, *Human Love*, 32.
[225] USCCB, *Stewardship*, 14.

this urgency can be lost to complacency, as Jesus asks, "if salt itself loses its taste, with what can its flavor be restored" (Lk 14:34)? Complacency can give way to fatigue or feelings of being demanded for giving "more" even though one may feel depleted.

Among the most serious obstacles to the stewardship way of life is simple selfishness. As Lanzrath explains, "Lack of love for God and neighbor leads to selfishness. Selfishness leads to an unwillingness to share. And our lack of willingness to share leads to a dying spiritual life."[226] Wichita adds, "Stewardship is not a selfish, "It's mine!" mentality, but a willingness to share what God has given for the good of the Church."[227]

Selfishness, coupled with a lack of historical knowledge, results in a sense of entitlement. Some people, not realizing, or simply ignoring the sacrifices of others, simply expect ostensible benefits of stewardship without playing into the system themselves. *Stewardship: A Disciple's Response* refers to this as "the calculus of self-interest: 'What's in it for me?'"[228] Related to this is the "give-get" mentality: "If I give my time, talent, and treasure then I get certain benefits." This reduces the practice of stewardship to minimalistic commitments that appear to be enforced by coercive incentives: "*Unless* you give "this much" then you *cannot* get such and such." As Clements says, "good stewards don't 'give to get.'"[229] Stewardship is not an exchange of goods; rather, it is a grateful response. The true "pay-out" is "the glory of God and the salvation of humanity (*Dei gloriam hominumque salute*)" (CIC, no.768).

Thus, the stewardship way of life is rooted in a spirituality of giving. Wichita's definition of stewardship contains the core understanding of stewardship which can be expounded upon in its various phrases. When a steward truly adopts the spirituality of giving they then take on the characteristics of a Christian steward. This life has many blessings as well as many obstacles. Aware of both blessings and obstacles allows one to live the life of stewardship by avoiding certain pitfalls and rejoicing in certain joys.

---

[226] Lanzrath, *Spirituality*, Lesson 3.
[227] CDOWK, *Formation*, 9.
[228] USCCB, *Stewardship*, 28.
[229] Clements, *Time, Talent and Treasure*, Kindle location 1440.

Chapter 5 - The Four Pillars of Stewardship

The great Cathedrals of the world cause one to look heavenward even as their marbled pillars connect their transcendent beauty to the earth. In the same way, the spirituality of giving causes us to look up to the inspirational beauty of the stewardship way of life, but there are four pillars of stewardship that ground this spirituality on practical action within the parish community. These four pillars are hospitality, prayer, formation, and service. [230]

As Wichita teaches, "The four pillars... invite parishioners to experience, witness, and live the stewardship way of life in response to their baptismal call to discipleship."[231] These pillars were a part of the early church community as seen in *Acts of the Apostles*,

> They devoted themselves to the teaching of the apostles (formation) and to the communal life (hospitality), to the breaking of the bread and to the prayers (prayer). Awe came upon everyone, and many wonders and signs (service) were done through the apostles. All who believed were together and had all things in common; they would sell their property and possessions and divide them among all according to each one's need (2:42-45).

The "wonders and signs" accomplished through the apostles can be compared to service because, as we saw earlier, the exercise of charisms always have as their aim, "the building up of the body of Christ" (Eph 4:12). The Decree on the Laity contains references to the pillars in relation to the family and the apostolate,

> The family will fulfill this mission if it appears as the domestic sanctuary of the Church by reason of the mutual affection of its members and the *prayer* that they offer to God in common, if the whole family makes itself a part of the liturgical worship of the Church, and if it provides active *hospitality* and promotes justice and other good works for the *service* of all the brethren in need (AA, 11, emphasis added).

It continues, "The apostolate can attain its maximum effectiveness only through a diversified and thorough *formation*" (AA, 28, emphasis added). Living the four pillars are one way the faithful carry out their baptismal offices of priest (prayer), prophet (formation) and king (hospitality and service; AA, 2).

---

[230] These pillars were the fourth goal of the 1985 Wichita listening sessions called *A People Gathered,* and subsequently a goal of the presbyteral gathering, called *Emmaus,* which inaugurated Wichita as a total stewardship diocese.

[231] CDOWK, *Pillars,* 6.

The Pillar of Hospitality

"Be hospitable to one another without complaining" (1 Pet 4:9). *Stewardship: A Disciple's Response* teaches that hospitality is first among the four pillars.[232] First, because, through it, people are treated with dignity, invited into a living community, and included as an integral part of its activity. Indeed, lack of hospitality ranks as one of the primary reasons that people either do not join, or leave, a community.[233] So Vatican II encourages, "The spirit of unity should be promoted in order that fraternal charity may be resplendent in the whole apostolate of the Church, common goals may be attained, and destructive rivalries avoided" (AA, 24). Indeed the Council charges pastors, "to reconcile differences of mentality in such a way that no one need feel himself a stranger in the community of the faithful" (PO, 9).

Hospitality, by its nature, must be personal.[234] It cannot be relegated to bulletin announcements, impersonal greetings, gimmicky actions, or programmatic structures. Clements defines hospitality as "'given to generous and cordial reception of guests' and 'offering a pleasant or sustaining environment.' In other words, hospitality is as much ambience as it is activity."[235] Hospitality is the atmosphere in which people are accepted for who they are, as they are, and generously included within the community. Wichita teaches that "hospitality... fosters a sense of 'belonging.' When parishioners experience a warm and sincere welcome, they in turn become open to give themselves to others."[236] And again, "This hospitality can, often times, provide the substance and glue necessary to keep individuals and families tied closely to their Catholic faith."[237]

Bob Hemberger, former Vicar General of the Diocese of Wichita, teaches that hospitality is fostered by the dual action of inspiration and invitation.[238] It begins by noticing new faces, is fostered by learning people's names, promoted through personal invitation, protected by avoiding cliques, progresses through patience, and culminates in acceptance.[239] Communicating service opportunities, creating social activities, following up on

---

[232] USCCB, *Stewardship*, 60.
[233] McGread, Sept 26, 2013, Blog.
[234] CDOWK, *Pillars,* 11.
[235] Clements, *Time, Talent, and Treasure*, Kindle Location 700-701.
[236] CDOWK, *Pillars,* 6.
[237] CDOWK, *Formation,* 18.
[238] Hemberger, *History,* audio.
[239] CDOWK, *Pillars,* 11.

parish sign-up lists, and reaching out to new parishioners, are all necessary steps for a parish to be vibrant in its hospitality.[240] Most importantly Wichita teaches that hospitality is the way in which people "seek the face of Christ in one another."[241]

The Pillar of Prayer

When jugglers juggle they keep their eyes fixed, not on the objects in their hands, but above them on an invisible spot through which the objects pass called an apex. Jesus Christ is the apex of Christian living. As jugglers keep their eyes fixed on the apex and pass their objects through it, Christians keep their "eyes fixed on Jesus," and pass all their activities through him in prayer (Heb 12:22). Wichita teaches that prayer is a participation in the priestly mission of Christ. "Beginning with the time they spend in liturgical worship and prayer, and flowing into the joy and patience with which they undertake their daily actions, parishioners participate in Christ's priestly mission."[242] Prayer is the "soul of the apostolate," as the famous spiritual writing calls it.[243] It is the privileged place where a Christian fulfills the summons, "Cast all your worries on him because he cares for you" (1 Pet 5:7). Vatican II echoes this,

> They should all remember that they can reach all men and contribute to the salvation of the whole world by public worship and prayer as well as by penance and voluntary acceptance of the labors and hardships of life whereby they become like the suffering Christ (2 Cor 4:10; Col 1:24; AA, 16).

Indeed, the offering of one's suffering for others is itself an act of stewardship. The prayer of a steward is both individual and communal.

Individually, Wichita says, "Prayer and sacraments dispose a soul to receive God's abundant graces, which are necessary to grow in holiness… Prayer purifies and intensifies the intention of a steward."[244] Thus, through prayer a steward strives for holiness. Gerber expounds,

> Holiness involves centering our lives on Jesus Christ; centering our lives on Jesus Christ centers our lives on the Eucharist; centering our lives on the Eucharist leads to discipleship; and discipleship demands

---

[240] Ibid., 12.

[241] Ibid., 11.

[242] Catholic Diocese of Wichita, *Characteristics of a Stewardship Parish in the Catholic Diocese of Wichita* (Wichita, KS: Catholic Diocese of Wichita, 1998), 2.

[243] Dom Jean-Baptiste Chautard, *The Soul of the Apostolate* (Trans. A Monk of Our Lady of Gethsemane) (Charlotte, NC: TAN Books, 1946), title.

[244] CDOWK, *Pillars*, 15.

active, practical day-to-day stewardship.[245]

Thus prayer fosters holiness, gratitude, and conversion expressed in life of virtue.[246]

The individual prayer life of a steward and the prayer life of the community intersect in Eucharist. In Wichita, this intersection is visible in the widespread practice of perpetual Eucharistic adoration. Gerber considers this discipline the primary source of success for stewardship and the increased vocations in Wichita.[247] Within Eucharistic adoration a steward not only bolsters one's own spiritual life but also enters into genuine intercessory prayer on behalf of one's family, community, society, and diocese. This intercessory nature of Eucharistic adoration begs God's grace to fall on all the 'fields' of the apostolate. Most importantly, adoration of the Eucharist engenders a sincere love for the sacrifice of the Mass itself.

Gerber states, "Sunday Mass Liturgy is the source and summit of our lives as faithful stewards... The Eucharist not only feeds us, but challenges us to share the gifts we have received with others."[248] Stewardship is a grateful response and the only adequate act of gratitude is to offer to God what he offered on our behalf, the sacrifice of his Son. Indeed, the very word Eucharist means thanksgiving.[249] Gerber tells us, "There is no higher way to personally encounter the Lord, to express our gratitude to him with praise than our full and active participation in the celebration of Mass."[250] This thanksgiving through the Eucharist then becomes a spring for stewardship activity as the *Code of Canon Law* states, "all the ecclesiastical works of the apostolate are closely connected with the Most Holy Eucharist and ordered to it" (CIC, no.897). And Wichita concludes, "The Eucharist not only feeds us, but challenges us to share the gifts we have received with others."[251]

The Pillar of Formation

Formation is not merely directed to programmatic application, nor to simple "how-to's" of ministries and outreaches. As Wichita says,

---

[245] Gerber, *Human Love*, 5.
[246] CDOWK, *Pillars,* 15, 16.
[247] Gerber, phone interview.
[248] Ibid., 15.
[249] CCC no. 1328.
[250] Gerber, email interview.
[251] CDOWK, *Pillars,* 16; CDOWK, *Formation,* 19.

Formation is a formidable task, involving education of mind and conversion of the heart. To *know* the 'stewardship way of life,' does not make one *live* a 'stewardship way of life.' Formation includes quality education, but the knowledge itself is not enough.[252]

Stewardship formation concerns both the individual and the community. [253]

Because stewardship cannot ultimately be separated from discipleship, formation of the individual includes conversion of mind and heart. Wichita states, "Educating parishioners in the spirituality and beauty of stewardship forms them to become the faithful disciples of Jesus to live their baptismal call."[254] As such, the giving of formation is a participation in the prophetic office of Christ.[255] The Bishops clarify that this formation should seamlessly unite the disciple's faith with the steward's works,

> Every diocese and parish should make education and formation for stewardship a major priority. This is vitally important today because (1) it helps individuals, families, and communities better understand what it means to follow Jesus in an affluent, consumer culture, and (2) it establishes an appropriate, scriptural basis for responding to the Church's growing need for human, physical, and financial resources.[256]

The *Decree on the Laity* also makes this point,

> Formation is demanded not only by the continuous spiritual and doctrinal progress of the lay person himself but also by the accommodation of his activity to circumstances varying according to the affairs, persons, and duties involved" (AA, 28).[257]

So as a disciple is formed to be a steward that steward in turn heightens the overall life of stewardship in a community.[258]

---

[252] CDOWK, *Pillars,* 18.

[253] The document goes on to say, "The long-term success and results of facilitating the stewardship way of life concept, the formation of grateful hearts within the parish, depends primarily, if not totally, upon four important factors. (1) The understanding, support, witness, articulation of and conversion to Christian stewardship by the pastor, coupled with: (2) The formation of an active, spiritually committed and vision driven parish stewardship council. Appropriately empowered, this council seeks to bring the message and concept of Christian stewardship to life within the lives of parishioners and the broad parish community, encompassing all parish ministries, organizations and activities. With the leadership of the pastor and his utilization of an active parish stewardship council, the parish: (3) Seeks, with the Eucharist as the focal point, to become the teacher of stewardship whereby the language, understanding and practice of stewardship is woven into the very fabric of the parish and the faith of its parishioners. (4) Cultivates that fertile soil within which the seeds of stewardship can be planted, tilled and harvested thus providing the invitation, encouragement, and opportunity for all to respond to their Baptismal call to discipleship. This assures their parish is viewed by all as a place of hospitality, prayer, formation and service" (CDOWK, *Formation,* 7).

[254] Ibid., 19.

[255] CDOWK, *Characteristics of a Stewardship Parish,* 3.

[256] USCCB, *Stewardship,* 51.

[257] The Decree goes on to say, "The formation for the apostolate presupposes a certain human and well-rounded formation adapted to the natural abilities and conditions of each lay person" (AA, 30).

[258] CDOWK, *Pillars,* 18.

The Bishops teach in *Stewardship: a Disciple's Response*, "A comprehensive approach to stewardship education and formation is essential if diocesan and parish communities truly wish to make stewardship a way of life for individuals, families, and communities."[259] This formation must be a stable part of a community and an essential aspect of its ministry especially in light of alternating pastors and changing demographics. Wichita further clarifies, "it is important for the language and practice of stewardship to become second nature and woven into the very fabric of the parish... homilies specifically targeting the subject of stewardship, should be planned and intentional."[260]

Stewardship formation can be direct or indirect. Direct formation occurs through education opportunities specifically designed to form in the stewardship way of life such as pastoral addresses, formation of parish councils, parishioner formation days, and participation in diocesan or national conferences. Indirectly, stewardship formation should be threaded into the various activities and education opportunities already occurring on a parish campus. Wichita explains, "Catholic schools, Parish Schools of Religion, youth ministry programs, adult education offerings and parish stewardship committees are wonderful and essential places where this faith formation begins."[261] Fr. Kenneth Vanhaverbeke, current director of the Office of Stewardship in Wichita, adds to this list, "marriage preparation, baptism formation, RCIA, Confirmation formation, second grade parents formation, parent meetings for sports."[262] Every facet of parish life can include stewardship formation in varying degrees.[263]

The Pillar of Service

Formation in stewardship culminates in the embracing of a spirituality of giving. This spirituality expresses itself in the Christian art of serving. St. Paul says, "Serve one another through love" (Gal 5:13) and Jesus came "not to be served but to serve" (Mt 20:28). Indeed, after Jesus finished washing the disciple's feet he taught, "I have given you a model to follow, so that as I have done for you, you should also do" (Jn 15:13). Thus imitating

---

[259] USCCB, *Stewardship*, 51.
[260] CDOWK, *Formation*, 19.
[261] CDOWK, *Pillars*, 18.
[262] Vanhaverbeke, 11.
[263] CDOWK, *Pillars*, 18, 19.

Jesus finds its highest expression in humble service. So St. Paul continues, "Bear one another's burdens, and so you will fulfill the law of Christ" (Gal 6:2). Through serving one another we offer our gifts to the needs of others thereby making one a minister of the Gospel. McGread poignantly states,

> We need to get back to the basics when we talk about stewardship. We need to realize that stewardship is not rocket science, but rather is something simple we all can grasp and understand. God will want to know how we took care of others' needs, and that's really what the stewardship way of life does. It provides us with the opportunity to care for another one's needs, just as Jesus has asked us to do. [264]

Such service is, in fact, an aspect of the "master's joy (Mt 14:21, 23)." Whether one is a bishop or a lay person, service is an aspect of the kingly mission of Christ.[265]

Wichita teaches, "At the very heart of Christian stewardship is the act of service."[266] This is because service is a participation in the mutual reciprocity that imitates the interior life of the Trinity discussed earlier. We have seen that at the heart of the Trinity is a mutual giving and receiving, an interchange of life and love. The Catechism explains, "God wills the *interdependence of creatures*... Creatures exist only in dependence on each other, to complete each other, in the service of each other" (CCC, no.340). The human person was created in the image and likeness of the interdependent relations of the Trinity. As such service is the act of giving and receiving among disciples in imitation of that Trinity. As Gerber says, "Stewardship opens the door to new avenues of giving and receiving."[267] Wichita further explains,

> A stewardship parish seeks to be that common faith community within which parishioners are invited and have the opportunity to serve and be served, giving, receiving and sharing their God-given giftedness. It is through the pillar of service at the parish or broader community level that a Christian steward is provided the opportunity to respond, in action, to his or her call to discipleship individually and or collectively.[268]

One benefit of this service is the sense of belonging it engenders both in the one serving and the one being served. Service operates out of the dual dignity spoken of earlier which communicates that, "I have something to give" and "you are worth my effort." Because of this, a community of service is a welcome home to all of its

---

[264] McGread, February 24th, 2013, in Catholic Stewardship Consultants, Inc. Blog, accessed, August 8, 2017, http://www.catholicsteward.com/category/msgr-mcgread/page/2/.

[265] CDOWK, *Characteristics of a Stewardship Parish*, 2. Pope St. John Paul II speaks of the Bishops service in terms of stewardship, "The power and authority of the bishops bears the mark of *diaconia* or *stewardship*,... Therefore the power that is found in the Church is to be understood as the power of being a servant" (CIC, p. 685).

[266] CDOWK, *Formation*, 19.

[267] Gerber, *Human Love*, 15.

[268] CDOWK, *Formation*, 20.

members.[269] A parish given over to service is vibrant in its life. The parish campus becomes a focal point of activity and a center of Christian living. All members find welcome and acceptance no matter how young or old. Persons with disabilities, or who are shut in, or are in hospitals are included through intercessory prayer as well outreach ministries. Finally, as with the lay apostolate, communities are called to serve the wider secular and diocesan community as well as the Church universal.[270]

So the four pillars describe the practical actions necessary to live the stewardship way of life as a parish community. While the spirituality of giving, contained within the definition of stewardship, inspires minds and hearts with the beauty of stewardship, the four pillars of hospitality, prayer, formation, and service, describe the practical actions a parish community takes to live stewardship. These four pillars create the context in which individual parishioners can "share their gifts" of time, talent, and treasure in love of God and neighbor.

---

[269] CDOWK, *Pillars*, 22.
[270] Ibid.

Chapter 6 - Three Areas of Giving[271]

As we have already seen, you cannot give what you do not have. We have also seen that stewardship is founded upon spirituality of giving, freely, without guilt or coercion.[272] A question can be asked, "*What* does a steward have to offer?" The answer is: time, talent, and treasure. These are the gifts we share in mutual reciprocity.[273] Or as *Living Life as God Intended It* explains, stewardship, "enables parishioners to approach their Savior, their pastor, and their neighbors with their hands full."[274]

Importantly, it is not time, talent, OR treasure; but time, talent, AND treasure. As Wichita teaches,

Only with His gift of life, with the rising and setting of His created sun, do we have the hours of each day to spend as we choose. Only with His gift of talents and skills that we cultivate and apply, are we able to work and play. Only with His bountiful generosity of these skills he creates in us, and the circumstances of life in which He places us, are we able to acquire the monetary income and material possessions that we have. True stewardship means giving back to God proportionately, sacrificially and generously in not one, but all three of these areas. Each area is an integral part of ourselves; to hold onto any of them is to hold back from giving ourselves over completely to our Father, as Jesus did.[275]

Stewardship requires discernment and conversion from the "calculus of self-interest" to an attitude of gratitude expressed in gift.[276] The Bishops teach young adults,

For your own development as a Catholic steward, it helps to spend time in prayer and reflection to recognize your gifts from God. Then discover how best to use those gifts for the benefit of others—and of course, invite others to discern and share their gifts, too.[277]

Discernment of gifts in a parish happens within the *annual stewardship renewal*, which is a yearly commitment of each parishioner to give their time, talent, and treasure. Ideally, this renewal should be seen as a meditation on sharing one's giftedness, not as an imposition or external obligation.

The Gift of Time

Time is the great equalizer: every human person has the exact same amount: 24 hours, 1,440 minutes, 86,400 seconds a day. The question concerning time isn't whether or not we have enough time to give, it is a

---

[271] CDOWK, *Characteristics of a Stewardship Parish*, 6.

[272] USCCB, *Stewardship*, 55.

[273] Ibid., 6.

[274] St. Francis of Assisi Parish, *Living*, 3.

[275] Ibid.

[276] CDOWK, *Pillars*, 15.

[277] USCCB, *Young Adults*, 2.

matter of prioritizing the time we have. According to current studies the average American adult spends per month 185 hours watching televised shows, 27 hours on the internet, and 35 hours connected online through their phone.[278] Yet the same adult averages 7 hours a month in worship[279] A question of discernment can be asked, "If time were money, is it 'spent' wisely?"

Clements comments, "For Christians, time is simply a way to measure God's great gift of life."[280] And it is important to keep this gift in perspective. The average lifespan of the human person in the US is 78.8 years.[281] If years were millimeters that would be less than the width of this paper. However, eternity is without end. All time must be evaluated in terms of eternity. *Stewardship: A Disciple's Response* teaches, "How we spend our time is perhaps the clearest indication of our progress in a life of Christian discipleship."[282]

Wichita states "to be good stewards of time – knowing, loving, and serving God – means spending time with God, with family, with work, with our parish and community, and with relaxation."[283] In terms of stewardship time is closely associated to prayer and service.[284] Prayer is the prime gift of time.[285] *Stewardship: A Disciple's Response* states,

> Part of what is involved here for Catholics is a stewardship of time, which should include setting aside periods for family prayer, for the reading of Scripture, for visits to the Blessed Sacrament, and for attendance at Mass during the week whenever this is possible.[286]

Vatican II encourages time to be spent in spiritual exercises, spiritual sacrifices, adoration, and even praying the Divine Office (LG, 34; *Sancrosanctum Concilium* (SC), 100).

While the handbook of stewardship is the Bible the "school of stewardship" is the Mass.[287] As Vatican II teaches, "The sacraments, however, especially the most holy Eucharist, communicate and nourish that charity

---

[278] Loicey, 4. Quoted sources from Nielsen Media Research, 2014, "How smartphones are changing Consumers' Daily Routines Around the Globe," February 24, 2014; Kaiser Family Foundation Study: "Generation M2: Media in the Lives of 8-to18-Year-Olds," January 2010; Bureau of Labor Statistics, "American Time Use Survey," June 22, 2011.

[279] McGread, Sept, 8th, 2010, Blog.

[280] Clements, *Time, Talent, and Treasure*, Kindle Location 1162.

[281] Larry Copeland, "Life expectancy in the USA his a record high," *USA Today*, October 8th, 2014, accessed August 11, 2017, https://www.usatoday.com/story/news/nation/2014/10/08/us-life-expectancy-hits-record-high/16874039/.

[282] USCCB, *Stewardship*, 66.

[283] CDOWK, *Characteristics of a Stewardship Parish*, 6

[284] Ibid., 7; Zech, *Best Practices*, 13.

[285] CDOWK, *Characteristics of a Christian Steward*, 11.

[286] USCCB, *Stewardship*, 28.

[287] CDOWK, *Formation*, 18.

which is the soul of the entire apostolate", from which "the faithful are to derive the true Christian Spirit" (AA, 3, LG, 33; SC 14). What we offer in the Eucharist is not merely bread and wine, but our very selves. *Stewardship: A Disciple's Response* illustrates how the Mass imparts this Christian Spirit, "As the elements of bread and wine are changed into the Body and Blood of Christ through the action of the Spirit, we also become more deeply transformed as disciples and stewards."[288] Lanzrath emphasized the Mass as a "holy exchange of gifts; my gift of self in exchange for God's gift of self."[289]

There is a connection between the "sacred service (*leitourgia*)" of 2 Cor 9:12 and the liturgy of the Church. Earlier we saw that *leitourgia* stood both for sacred service as well as a financial gift. The catechism echoes this,

> The word 'liturgy' originally meant a 'public work' or a 'service in the name of/on behalf of the people.' Through the liturgy Christ, our redeemer and high priest, continues the work of our redemption in, with, and through his Church….In the New Testament the word "liturgy" refers not only to the celebration of divine worship but also to the proclamation of the Gospel and to active charity (1069 - 1070).

What Jesus returns to us is a participation in his life, uniting us in one body, propelling us to serve God and neighbor through the sharing of our talents.

The Gift of Talent

Wichita defines stewardship as a sharing of "God's gifts." Earlier we spent a considerable amount of effort to relate the term gifts to the spiritual notion of *charisma*. Several points were made. The gifts of time, talent, and treasure, while referring to natural gifts, need also to refer to spiritual gifts, charisms. Charisms are supernatural endowments, either building on natural talents or are directly given by the Spirit. Yet spiritual gifts themselves are but the kaleidoscope presence of the one Holy Spirit. This Holy Spirit produces within the people of God one communion or *koinonia*. This *koinonia* bears within it both the meaning of a spiritual union of persons as well as a physical sharing of material resources. Thus a circle is completed from time, talent, and treasure, through spiritual gifts, to the Spirit himself, who creates communion, which is shared precisely in the gifts of time, talent, and treasure.

---

[288] USCCB, *Stewardship*, 3.
[289] Lanzrath, *Spirituality*, Lesson 4.

Vatican II captures this connection of physical gift and unity, "Through the common sharing of gifts and through the common effort to attain fullness in unity, the whole and each of the parts receive increase" (LG, 13). And again it says, the faithful "should not cease to develop earnestly the qualities and talents bestowed on them in accord with these conditions of life, and they should make use of the gifts which they have received from the Holy Spirit" (AA, 4).

However, a word needs to be said concerning natural talents, which are an essential part of the gifts God bestows upon his disciple's. *Stewardship: A Disciple's Response* teaches, "Stewardship of the gift of talent means nurturing, developing, and using the God-given abilities and characteristics that help to define 'who we are' as individual human persons."[290] Indeed the human person has many natural 'intelligences' that can be considered raw material for the life of stewardship. For example, Howard Gardner in his 1983 book *Frames of Mind: The Theory of Multiple Intelligences* posited seven expressions of intelligence in the human person: musical, spatial, linguistic, mathematical, kinesthetic, interpersonal, and intrapersonal.[291] In addition to an understanding of natural intelligences many parishes and dioceses' rely on the popular *Strengths Finders* analysis tool to help persons understand their natural abilities. This tool identifies thirty-four different "talents/themes/strengths."[292] Zech suggests,

> We should assess our strengths and determine how they might be used to help build the kingdom of God. These strengths could be an overt talent like sewing or painting or an internal skill such as organizing or listening. Each of us is gifted and can perform some action to help others.[293]

By identifying such strengths parishioners are then able to find a more fitting way to offer their stewardship.[294]

Wichita concludes,

---

[290] USCCB, *Stewardship*, 66.

[291] Howard Gardner, *Frames of Mind: The Theory of Multiple Intelligences* (New York, NY: Basic Books, 1983), Table of Contents.

[292] Tom Rath, founder of Strengths Finders, lists these as, "Achiever, activator, adaptability, analytical, arranger, belief, command, communication, competition, connectedness, consistency/fairness, context, deliberative, developer, discipline, empathy, focus, futuristic, harmony, ideation, inclusiveness/include, individualization, input, intellection, learner, maximizer, positivity, relator, responsibility, restorative, self-assurance, significance, strategic, woo." Tom Rath, *Strengths Finders 2.0* (New York, NY: Gallup Press, 2007), Table of Contents.

[293] Zech, *Best Practices*, 13.

[294] Clements elaborates on this saying, "Here are some questions we can ask ourselves to help identify our talents, interests, and abilities: 1. What is my occupation, vocation, or profession? 2. What additional skills, talents, or interests do I have? 3. What are my spare time hobbies? 4. What kinds of skills, talents, or abilities do my friends and family members tell me I have? 5. What are some specific needs in my community" (*Time, Talent, and Treasure*, Kindle Locations 1204-1208).

Stewards of talent recognize that using the abilities God has given them, whether with family, work, parish, or recreation, should serve Him by serving others... Beyond cultivating their own talents, good stewards also cultivate the talents of others.[295]

The Gift of Treasure

McGread was fond of saying, "You will never find a U-Haul behind a hearse." Jesus himself warned of being over attached to wealth. To the rich person who stored up grain for himself he said, "You fool, this night your life will be demanded of you and the things you have prepared, to whom will they belong" (Lk 12:20)? Wealth is a gift given to be of service to others. Money is like seed: when it is spread out, in the right conditions, and with the proper care, it springs forth new life. The stewardship way of life is not primarily about money. For example if a parish were to be totally destitute, living in abject poverty, the persons of that parish would still be called to stewardship. Stewardship is primarily about self-gift arising from gratitude for God's abundant gifts. Yet, our finances are one aspect of that self-gift.

Money, though it is needful in the life of a parish, is first a symbol of the self-gift that a disciple has already made. The giving of treasure is analogous to a sacramental. A sacramental, like a holy medal, is not a source of grace but a symbol of a grace given in Jesus Christ. So too, one's treasure is not the gift in itself, rather it is a symbol of the gift *of self* that one has already given. Lanzrath comments, "The giving of our money is, in fact, a giving of ourselves... representing the gift of our labor... our heart.. our life."[296] What we put in the basket, what is symbolized in the offering of bread and wine, is our very self.[297] Bishop Michael Jackels, former Bishop of Wichita, teaches,

> Whether or not you participate in the collection is going to have a consequence on how deeply you participate in the Eucharistic prayer and how fruitfully receiving Holy Communion is going to be for you. Because what I put into the basket is a concrete expression of my gift of self. That's the only gift I have to give. I can pull money out of my wallet. God can take that from me without asking me. But the one thing God can't take unless I give is my self, my gift of self, expressly as it is exercised by my will.[298]

The collection at Mass is primarily about giving of oneself; only secondarily is it about pragmatic or financial

---

[295] CDOWK, *Characteristics of a Stewardship Parish*, 7.
[296] Lanzrath, *Spirituality*, Lesson 4.
[297] Ibid.
[298] Most Reverend Michael O. Jackels, "The Spirituality of Stewardship: A Holy Exchange of Gifts," YouTube video, 3:24, posted by the Catholic Diocese of Wichita, April 2, 2010, accessed August 8, 2017, http://catholicdioceseofwichita.org/wichita-news/11480-bishop-talks-about-giving-of-self-at-mass-11480.

concerns.

Vatican II only spoke about physical giving twice and this in non-explicit terms. "They should especially make missionary activity their own by giving material or even personal assistance... It is a duty and honor for Christians to return to God a part of the good things that they receive from Him" (AA, 10). We see here the inference of treasure (material) and talents (personal assistance) with the addition of making 'a return to God' in gratitude for what he has given us.[299] The *Code of Canon law* adds, "The Christian faithful are obliged to assist with the needs of the Church so that the Church has what is necessary for divine worship, for the works of the apostolate and of charity, and for the decent support of ministers" (CIC, no.222; no.1261) and includes the need to support various appeals (CIC, no.1262).

Notice, specifically, the gift supports the apostolate. In other words, The motivator for giving generously arises from the Church's mission, "Go, therefore, and make disciples of all nations, baptizing them in the name of the Father, and of the Son, and of the holy Spirit" (Mt 28:19). This mission is carried out through evangelization. When people are inspired to take up their role in this mission they will also be inspired to grow in their generosity in giving their time, talent, and treasure.[300] At every moment stewardship must be a faith response to this mission - a response in trust.[301]

Stewards, motivated by mission and knowing they have a part to play, are called to give their first fruits.[302] This among the earliest lessons of the Bible: Abel gave of his first fruits and was blessed (Gen 4:3). Proverbs says, "Honor the Lord with your wealth, with first fruits of all your produce; then will your barns be filled with grain, with new wine your vats will overflow" (3:9-10). Clements comments "'First-fruits' in today's vernacular is ten percent of gross earnings or, in IRS terminology, adjusted gross income."[303] Zech explains,

---

[299] This is referred to as giving back because "when we tithe we are returning 10% of something that ultimately 100% belongs to God anyway. But this giving back is an act of worship and trust in our generous and abundant God who wants us to keep and enjoy 90% of all His blessings" (CDOWK, *Tithing*, 6).

[300] See Appendix B for Zech's "Seven Things the Catholic Church can do to Increase Contributions."

[301] The Bishops encourage "...a willingness to trust that if stewardship is taught and accepted as a faith response, urgently needed human, physical, and financial resources will follow" (USCCB, *Stewardship*, 50). They further admonish that all respect "...the responsibility to make sure that all leadership development and fund-raising efforts are consistent with, and reinforce, the theology and practice of stewardship as outlined in the pastoral letter and this manual" (Ibid, 52).

[302] "This praise and worship is not by returning what is left over; instead it is giving off the top, the first fruits, the tithe" (Gerber, email interview).

[303] Clements, *Time, Talent, and Treasure*, Kindle Locations 1424-1425.

Planning to return the first portion of our earnings to God is a way of showing our gratitude and commitment to stewardship. Tithing, giving the first 10% of what we receive, is the traditional (Biblical) guideline of how to give to God. Stewardship calls us to give in proportion to our blessings by sharing a percentage of our gifts. However, it also means being responsible stewards of the other 90%, or what is left, and using it in a way befitting a God-centered person if we are truly committed to embracing stewardship as a way of life.[304]

The prophet Malachi says, "Bring the whole tithe into the storehouse, that there may be food in my house, and try me in this, says the Lord of hosts: shall I not open for you the floodgates of heaven, to pour down blessings upon you without measure" (3:10). God cannot be outdone in generosity, as his own word testifies.

Stewardship: A Disciple's Response, rather than using the word "tithe," refers to maximum giving, or "giving according to our means."[305] The Bishops document explains, "Stewardship is not minimum giving. It is maximum giving. That means giving as much as we can, as often as we can, from the heart as a faith response."[306] The 10% that is encouraged in the stewardship way of life is an explicit standard to which the Christian faithful are challenged. Many parishes encourage this giving through pledges, discussed earlier with 2 Cor 9:5-15. This practice sets personal goals for a "total commitment to stewardship that is planned, proportionate, and sacrificial."[307] Beginning to give a tenth of one's income is difficult. The amount of one's tithe is arrived at by discernment through prayer and reflection motivated by a sincere desire to give out of one's need. As St. Paul says, "Each on must do as he has purposed in his heart" (NAS, 2 Cor 9:7). Then, over time, persons are encouraged to incrementally increase their giving to 10% through their pledge.[308]

In addition to ordinary forms of giving (maximum giving, tithe, and pledge) there are also extraordinary forms of giving, either directly or indirectly. Direct giving refers to appeals, planned giving, capital campaigns and endowments. The Bishops' document continues, "The primary advantage of direct fundraising is its

---

[304] Zech, *Best Practices*, 13.
[305] USCCB, *Stewardship*, 67
[306] Ibid, *67*.
[307] Ibid., 54. Bishop Gerber cautions, "I have resistance to the term "sacrificial giving" – there was a priest who promoted in this way... it just died. "Equal sacrifice" does not fit well with stewardship. I think it takes away the fundamental spirituality of stewardship. It puts the sacrifice ahead of the discernment. It changes the motive. "sacrifice" is negative. The motive of the widow was not sacrificial giving – it was the spiritual act of giving. It was a spirituality – it was the heart she gave – it was an act of worship" (Gerber, phone interview).
[308] Wichita teaches, "If you increase your giving every year by at least ½ percent or more, you will eventually reach a full tithe of10%. It is usually suggested that you give 8% to your parish and 2% combined to any other charities which touch your heart" (*Tithing*, 11).

emphasis on building a strong, personal relationship between the donor and the organization that it is seeking

support."[309] All development efforts in a stewardship parish must protect the faith-based response of

stewardship free of coercion or command.[310] Wichita teaches,

> Fundraising violates the principles of stewardship when:
> a) It replaces the tithe or portion of a tithe of a parishioner;
> b) A parish becomes dependent upon fundraising to meet ordinary operating expenses;
> c) The event does not help the faithful gratefully recognize and receive God's gifts and allow them to share them in love of God and neighbor.
> d) Presents the Church in an unfavorable light.[311]

Indirect fundraisers such as auctions, galas, bingo, magazine sells, baking sells etc. can easily be inimical to these

stewardship principles. They also tend to be virtually interminable.[312] Caution and reticence is necessary when

discerning indirect fundraisers.

Our God is a lavish giver (Ps. 112:9). Stewardship is our way of imitating God in his lavish gift. We who

have freely been given every physical thing must share those physical things with God and neighbor. Wichita

describes the benefits of tithing,

> You realize the difference between what you need and what you want... eliminate the endless clutter of material wants... stop being "consumed by consumerism" and "possessed by your possessions" and begin to slow down and prioritize not only how you spend your money but also how you spend your time...find enjoyment in simple pleasures – especially time to deepen your relationships with God, with loved ones and with your community... Ultimately, those who tithe feel the practice brings more joy, more peace, more contentment and more balance to their lives[313]

Jesus Christ, who gave us his very self, asks us to share our own self in return. The tithe is about the need to

give. We give because, by it, we imitate God who has given us everything.

In conclusion, everyone has something to offer. Everyone has something to give. Every human person has

a varying measure of time, talent, and treasure. Through discernment one is able learn from God how much of

each of these one is able to give. While it is true each of us differ in our ability to give of these according to our

---

[309] USCCB, *Stewardship*, 64.

[310] Wichita teaches, "When evaluating any development opportunity, a simple reflection on the following questions might be beneficial: a. Does this event/process/appeal better form the grateful response of a Christian disciple? b. Does this event/process/appeal detract from the sacrificial, generous and proportional giving of a steward" (CDOWK, *Relationship*, 12).

[311] CDOWK, *Relationship*, 11.

[312] USCCB, *Stewardship*, 64.

[313] Ibid, 10

state in life, it is also true that we are called to share something of each as a grateful response to God's

abundant gifts. And, as the Parable of the Talents reminds us, we will be accountable for our stewardship.

Chapter 7 - Accountability of a Christian Steward

Accountability is a part of our society. Whether it is a restaurant opinion card, a student's report card, or a professional employee review, accountability is the way people know what is expected of them and it summons them to succeed. The Bishops continue, "Evidently, good stewards understand that they are to share with others what they have received, that this must be done in a timely way, and that God will hold them accountable for how well or badly they do it."[314] Jesus himself, in the parable of the talents, reminds us that we will be held accountable for our responsibilities. St. Paul adds, "Each of us will give an account of himself to God" (Rom 14:12). In other words, the mission of Jesus Christ is not an ethereal idea. It has concrete expectations with concrete outcomes.

These concrete expectations provide people with a standard of living. McGread asserts that "people are looking for standards in life."[315] Standards provide a benchmark against which one can measure personal growth. The stewardship way of life provides a disciple clear standards for which to strive. The very definition of a 'steward' articulated in *Stewardship: A Disciple's Response* includes the call to standards: a steward is "...one who receives God's gifts... and returns them with increase to the Lord."[316]

Parishioner Accountability

A 'parishioner' is defined as a person who, "registers and participates regularly and actively in the liturgical and social life of the parish community... [and] commits to share his/her gifts of time, talent and treasure, which are expressions of the very gift of self."[317] In Wichita parishioners are encouraged to enter into accountability explicitly through the *Parish Family Agreement (PFA)*. This agreement states,

> I acknowledge that all that I have is a gift from God, and that I must be a good steward through my example and my actions. I ask the support of my parish in nurturing my faith as I strive to live the stewardship way of life. I pledge my cooperation with the parish and its ministries, and, if I have children, I will make every effort to supervise their commitment as well.[318]

There are six commitments made in the *Parish Family Agreement*.[319]

---

[314] Ibid.
[315] McArdle, *Grateful and Giving,* 13-15.
[316] USCCB, *Stewardship*, 9.
[317] CDOWK, *Formation*, 7.
[318] St. Francis of Assisi Parish, *Parish Family Agreement*, 1.

1. Make a life-long commitment to practice stewardship as a way of life.

2. Participate at Mass on Sundays and Holy Days, ideally in your parish.

3. Practice the faith in the workplace, the home, the classroom, and in civic life.

4. Support and cooperate with the religious education programs of the parish: adult faith formation, Catholic School, PSR, sacramental preparation, RCIA, etc.

5. Participate in parish ministries, activities, and organizations through your contribution of time and talent.

6. Support ministries of the Catholic Church by pledging and tithing sacrificially to the parish (with a goal of 8% of family income to the parish and 2% to other charities of your choice).

Let's turn our attention to each of these.

1. *Make a life-long commitment to practice stewardship as a way of life*. Stewardship must be life-long.

Stewardship: A Disciple's Response teaches,

> Stewardship involves a lifelong process of study, reflection, prayer and action. To make stewardship a way of life for individuals, families, parishes, and dioceses requires a change of heart and a new understanding of what it means to follow Jesus without counting the cost.[320]

Stewardship is life-long because the mission of the church, to evangelize all people, is life-long. One is committed to this mission by virtue of one's discipleship. Yet, the way in which we participate in this mission changes according to the various seasons of our life. The time, talent, and treasure, a person had at one period in life are different at another period of life. Young or old, healthy or sick, rich or poor, agile or disabled, all of us are called to participate in one way or another. Nor is it question of quantity, "how much" a person can give. It's a matter of gift: whatever one can give is needful to give; even if the gift is offering one's sufferings in union with Christ's (Col 1:24).

2. *Participate at Mass on Sundays and Holy Days, ideally in your parish*. St. Paul says we "exist for the praise of his glory" (Eph 1:12). And the third commandment says, "Keep holy the Lord's day" (Ex 20:8). The steward recognizes that participation at Sunday Mass is the preeminent way for one to express gratitude to God for all he has done for us (Is 63:7). The Psalm asks, "How can I repay the Lord for all the great good done for

---

[319] Ibid.
[320] USCCB, *Stewardship*, 51.

me? I will raise the cup of salvation and call on the name of the Lord" (116:12-13). Stewards recognize that their absence at Mass is tangibly felt.

Many in today's society ask, "why do I have to go to Mass on Sunday?" The answer is found within the life of the Trinity: *the God who is a Community of Persons desires to be worshipped in a community of persons.* Community worship is a participation in the image and likeness of God. Christians worship God on Sunday, or the Saturday night vigil. St. Ignatius of Antioch, in the year 110 a.d. taught "we live in accordance with the Lord's Day (Sunday), on which [Jesus] arose... so that we may be found to be disciples of Jesus Christ."[321] And even before that the Book of Hebrews explicitly states, "We should not stay away from our assembly, as is the custom of some, but encourage one another" (10:25). Even in the early Church some stayed away from the assembly! Stewards prioritize Sunday Mass every Sunday.

3. *Practice the faith in the workplace, the home, the classroom, and in civic life.* A steward's life of faith is not relegated to the Church or to the home. Stewards evangelize in every 'field' of the apostolate. Jesus has sent us out as "lambs among wolves" (Lk 10:3). Faith is not compartmentalized into one period of a week. A disciple does not shirk from a professing faith in word nor living it in deed.

4. *Support and cooperate with the religious education programs of the parish: adult faith formation, Catholic School, PSR, sacramental preparation, RCIA, etc.* While we have already discussed formation earlier, and need not be repeated, what needs to be explicitly stated is this: as goes adult education so goes stewardship. Pope St. John Paul II taught that adult education is "...the principal form of catechesis... The Christian community cannot carry out a permanent catechesis without the direct and skilled participation of adults, whether as receivers or as promoters of catechetical activity" (43).

5. *Participate in parish ministries, activities, and organizations through your contribution of time and talent.* We are all called to "bear one another's burdens" (Gal 6:2). We do this by our generous service to one another. Each of us have a role in carrying one another burdens; and no one can transfer their responsibility to someone else. So St. Paul adds, "bear your *own* share of the burden of the Gospel" (2 Tim 1:8). No one is

---

[321] St. Ignatius of Antioch, *Letter to the Magnesians*, in *The Apostolic Fathers in English, 3rd* ed., trans. and ed. Michael W. Holmes, (Grand Rapids: Baker, 2006), 9:1.

excluded from the invitation of the mission of Jesus Christ. When we yoke ourselves to Jesus and, through him, to one another, we all share the burdens of life together (Mt 11:29-30).

6. *Support ministries of the Catholic Church by pledging and tithing sacrificially to the parish (with a goal of 8% of family income to the parish and 2% to other charities of your choice).* Finances are a pressure upon all whether one is the head of a house or the head of a parish. Talking about money is an immediate stressor. Yet the truth is this: physical creatures owe a physical return to the Lord. Tithing back to God operates from two truths. First, we have been given 100% of everything, even God's own Son, so in gratitude we give back out of respect for God's gifts. Second, a tithe is an external act of an interior trust. St. Paul says, "He who did not spare his own Son... will he not also give us everything else along with him" (Rom 8:32). We can trust God.

In the final analysis only three of these six can be quantifiably measured. Three essential questions accountability can be asked of every steward:

1. Am I attending Mass on Sundays and Holy Days of Obligation?

2. Am I participating in service opportunities at the parish?

3. Am I making and keeping an honest pledge of treasure?

These three questions form the substance of any dialogue concerning accountability.

Pastor Accountability

Pastors and laity are mutually dependent upon one another as "co-workers in the various forms and modes of the apostolate" as Vatican II teaches (LG 32, AA 10, 24; AA, 33). Vatican II continues,

> For their pastors know how much the laity contribute to the welfare of the entire Church. They also know that they were not ordained by Christ to take upon themselves alone the entire salvific mission of the Church toward the world. On the contrary they understand that it is their noble duty to shepherd the faithful and to recognize their ministries and charisms, so that all according to their proper roles may cooperate in this common undertaking with one mind (LG, 30).

Indeed, Vatican II's teaching must be remembered, "The ordained ministry or *ministerial* priesthood is at the service of the baptismal priesthood" (LG, 10).

Not only laity, but pastors as well are called to be accountable. All six commitments outlined above are equally applicable to pastors and all priests. In addition, priests should not fail to study diligently Canons 518-

537 to live up to the standards of stewardship expected of them by the Church. Gerber bluntly states, "The simple fact is that the pastor is the key to the success of the stewardship effort."[322]

A pastor's accountability as a steward begins with his own personal commitment to the stewardship way of life.[323] This commitment comes by way of conversion. Wichita teaches, "The personal conversion (of the pastor) as well as his visible support for the message is needed to teach the stewardship way of life throughout the parish and wider community."[324] In this way, the pastor will lead by example, offering his own first fruits even as the Levites offered "a tithe of the tithe" (Num 18:26).[325] He is to preach on stewardship, not only in the homily, but in every avenue of formation discussed above.[326] He should be present to God in prayer, and present to his people in hospitality. Wichita teaches, "The pastor serves best by making himself available to parishioners to meet spiritual needs. Being present with parishioners in times of illness, bereavement, loneliness and confusion leave lasting impressions."[327] A pastor's presence is exponentially helped by memorizing the names of his parishioners. Finally, a pastor exercises his stewardship when he empowers his committees to take true leadership. Vatican II asks parish pastors to be

> ...willing to make use of the laity's prudent advice. Let them confidently assign duties to the laity in the service of the Church, allowing them freedom and room for action. Further, let pastors encourage the laity so that they may undertake tasks on their own initiative (LG, 37).[328]

The stewardship way of life owes its success to highly motivated lay leadership inspired by various ecclesial movements. Such movements should be encouraged by the pastor.

People of all ages desire standards in life. A young athlete obeys a coach who challenges him or her to a greater level of success. Business men and women receive annual reviews to enhance performance. Christians

---

[322] Gerber, *Human Love,* 29.

[323] The Bishops emphasize this point saying, "To be successful, stewardship education requires the bishop or pastor to make a complete, constant, personal, and official commitment to stewardship as a constitutive element of Christian discipleship" (USCCB, *Stewardship*, 51).

[324] CDOWK, *Pillars,* 18.

[325] St. Francis of Assisi Parish, *Living,* 3; McArdle, *Grateful and Giving,* 120.

[326] CDOWK, *Pillars,* 18.

[327] Ibid., 22.

[328] The same document also states, "The laity have the right, as do all Christians, to receive in abundance from their spiritual shepherds the spiritual goods of the Church, especially the assistance of the word of God and of the sacraments. They should openly reveal to them their needs and desires with that freedom and confidence which is fitting for children of God and brothers in Christ. They are, by reason of the knowledge, competence or outstanding ability which they may enjoy, permitted and sometimes even obliged to express their opinion on those things which concern the good of the Church" (LG, 37).

use the Beatitudes as a measure by which to grow in holiness. Thus stewards, both laity and clergy, use the six

commitments of the stewardship way of life as standards to achieve a life of self-gift.

Chapter 8 - A Stewardship Parish

Just as a parish is made up of individual parishioners, a stewardship parish is made up of individuals committed to the stewardship way of life. The greater the commitment individuals have to stewardship the more a parish can be truly be called a stewardship parish. A stewardship parish is one in which pastors and laity alike are united in shared discipleship expressed in an evangelizing way that encourages persons to not only embrace the Gospel but take up their proper role within the life of the parish family.[329] Wichita explains,

> A stewardship parish, within the unique demographics of each, seeks through regular participation in the celebration of the Eucharist, to spiritually form the lives of its parishioners. Parishioners, in turn, are invited, encouraged, sent forward and given the opportunity to become actively engaged and involved. This invitation, opportunity, and involvement then tends to facilitate a real life experience and sense of hospitality, prayer, formation, and service within the parish community.[330]

It continues, "The parish exists to evangelize. The parish is an intentional community charged with growing in faith, sharing faith and transforming the world in faith."[331] Thus a parish, in order to be a stewardship parish, must subordinate stewardship to discipleship and make discipleship missionary in its practice. This means that a parish needs to be in a constant state of conversion to Jesus Christ through the kerygma.

Perhaps it could be said that a parish needs to see itself as an ecclesial movement.[332] An ecclesial movement is "...a concrete ecclesial reality with predominantly lay membership, a faith journey and Christian witness which bases its own pedagogical method on a precise charism given to the person of the founder in specific circumstances and ways."[333] While this concept is not generally associated to parishes, when it comes to the clarity of the stewardship way of life and its structure of accountability, could a parish not be seen through the lens of an ecclesial movement?

Recently, during World Youth Day, Polish Bishops asked Pope Francis,

Holy Father, our pastoral work is based largely on the traditional model of the parish community,

---

[329] See Appendix C for a list of best and worst practices in renewing parish stewardship.

[330] CDOWK, *Formation*, 7.

[331] Catholic Diocese of Wichita, *Guidelines for Parish Pastoral Councils* (Wichita, KS: Catholic Diocese of Wichita, Date unknown), 7.

[332] Monica Pope made this comment during a class presentation for *Models of the New Evangelization* under the professorship of Dr. Ralph Martin. August 2015.

[333] Pope St. John Paul II, *Message of Pope John Paul II for the World Congress of Ecclesial Movements and New Communities* (Vatican: Libreria Editrice Vaticana, 1998), no.4.

centered on the sacramental life... Is there a specific way you can encourage us to build up the Church community in our world fruitfully, joyfully and with a missionary spirit? [334]

Pope Francis' response was very clear and direct and helps us think deeply of what the identity of a stewardship parish should be:

> I would like to stress one thing: the parish remains valid! The parish must remain. It is a structure that we must not discard; it is the home of God's People. The problem is how the parish is organized! There are parishes... who scare people off. Parishes with closed doors... But there also parishes with open doors, parishes where when someone comes to ask a question, they are told: "Come in, make yourself at home, what can we do for you?" And someone listens to them patiently, because caring for the people of God requires patience; it takes effort!
> Managing a parish takes effort nowadays... The Lord has asked us to get a little tired, to work and not to rest... A parish is exhausting if it is well organized. The renewal of the parish has to be a constant concern... It has to remain a place of creativity, a reference point, a mother, where inventiveness finds expression. When a parish does all this, it becomes a missionary disciple, a parish that goes forth. [335]

A parish's missionary efforts can only as big as its parishioner's gift of stewardship. As resources of time, talent, and treasure increase outreach can expand. As those same resources decrease a parish feels the pinch of constriction. Yet parishes are not in the business of making a profit. They are in the business proclaiming the Gospel. As such, a stewardship parish will frequently feel the sting of stretching itself to the limits to provide for this mission.

Wichita teaches that there are eight characteristics of a stewardship parish.[336]

1. Parishioners have the opportunity to grow in union with God and one another, through the Eucharist, by liturgical worship, prayer, education, and service.

2. An active Stewardship Committee is in place.

3. Parishioners give proportionately, generously, and sacrificially of their time, talent and treasure.

4. A mission statement, pastoral plan and supporting structure are in place.

5. Stewardship education is ongoing.

---

[334] Pope Francis, *Meeting with Polish Bishops: Address of His Holiness Pope Francis* (given as a response to questions posed by the Polish Bishop at meeting in Krakow, July 27, 2016), accessed August 14, 2017, https://w2.vatican.va/content/francesco/en/speeches/2016/july/documents/papa-francesco_20160727_polonia-vescovi.html.

[335] Ibid.

[336] CDOWK, *Characteristics of a Stewardship Parish*, 1.

6. There is an annual stewardship renewal and follow-up process in place.

7. Special fund raising needs, when necessary, are conducted within the definition, spirituality and context of the Church's teaching and practice of stewardship.

8. Planned giving (the stewardship of assets) and endowment awareness are promoted.

In the same way a steward is held accountable to three concrete questions, a parish is to be held accountable to its mission outlined in this list.[337] There are several benefits of a parish being stewardship parish. It is more hospitable and welcoming. It prioritizes the spiritual growth of its people. And it invites parishioners into a life of service through "proportionate, generous and sacrificial giving."[338]

Steps to Inaugurate Stewardship in Your Parish

While it is outside the scope of this paper to provide the "how to's" of starting stewardship within a parish, Gerber does provide a succinct list that points one in the right direction.[339] Gerber lists:

1. Start with prayer... Eucharistic and Marian Devotion.

2. Prayerfully discern four to six couples with whom you can pray, explore stewardship, and allow planning to emerge.

3. When the time comes communicate beyond this group...do it well.

4. Make sure that you are in concert with the Bishop and supportive of his vision for the diocese.

5. When presenting treasure situate Church support in the broader context of what it means to be a disciple. Resist the temptation to put treasure first, regardless of pressing capital or budgetary needs.

6. In the emergence of a pastoral plan... be sure to include annual renewal.

7. Trust in the Gospel principles of stewardship and trust in edging forward in your own personal conversion.

Several authors and books listed in the bibliography will treat this topic at length.

Stewardship and Catholic Schools

Among the many fruits of stewardship experienced in Wichita, the one with the most notoriety is the

---

[337] USCCB, *Stewardship*, 68.
[338] CDOWK, *Characteristics of a Stewardship Parish*, 1.
[339] Gerber, *Human Love*, 31.

provision of Catholic education as one mission of the parish. Catholic education in Wichita is not "free." While it is true, as a mission of the parish, individual parish families do not pay tuition, it is equally true that catholic schools require anywhere from 65% to 75% of a parish's total budget. Not to mention, while families are free of tuition, there are fees for registration, meal programs, and extracurricular activities. The real "cost" of Catholic education is the engaged and active stewardship of the entire parish and diocese, not just families with children in school.

Canon 798 states, "Parents are to entrust their children to those schools which provide a Catholic education. If they are unable to do this, they are obliged to take care that suitable Catholic education is provided for their children outside the schools." It needs to be noted, that catholic schools are one ministry among many in which the proclamation of the Gospel is provided by the parish. P.S.R., R.C.I.A., adult education, young adult ministry, etc. are various "hues" of Catholic education. Even if a parish were without a Catholic school it would still invest in utilities, buildings, insurance, supplies, desks, employees, etc for catholic education. Simply because Catholic schools take more financial and personal resources does not mean other ministries suffer where a Catholic school exists. Where a school does exist it should be clearly understood by all, especially by families, that a community is not primarily a Catholic school with a parish attached, but is a *parish* with a Catholic school as one of its many ministries. Catholic schools, both grade schools and high schools, are always, and in every way, a mission and ministry of the entire parish family and the entire diocese.[340]

The Catholic Diocese of Wichita is the only diocese in the world in which all Catholic schools follow this model. Each Catholic school in the diocese is funded primarily through the tithe collected on Sundays.[341] Catholic High schools are funded by the parish through a direct support paid to the Catholic School Office for each youth a parish sponsors. This direct support is approximately $3600.00 per student. It is because Catholic schools are funded as a mission of the parish, supported through the tithe, that they are tax exempt. But this tax exempt status is seriously threatened when pastors employ methods of accountability that do not align with the faith-based reality of the stewardship way of life.[342]

---

[340] CDOWK, *Suggested Talking Points for Pastors & Catholic School Families in the Parish Grade School.*
[341] However, this does not exclude the possibility of capitalizing on government programs, tax incentives, grants, or matching-gifts.

The Church has always maintained that parents are to be the "first… and best of teachers" in the ways of faith.[343] As Vatican II states, "Parents must be acknowledged as the first and foremost educators of their children. Their role as educators is so decisive that scarcely anything can compensate for their failure in it" (*Gravissimum Educationis*, 3). In a particular way, Wichita teaches that the catholic school is "…a partnership among the family, the parish, and the school."[344] This partnership requires the active involvement of families who elect to participate in this benefit. For families living active stewardship in all three, not just one, of the areas of time, talent, and treasure, "the parish will make every effort to assist them."[345] However, complacency, fatigue, entitlement, lack of historical knowledge, and the many other obstacles enumerated throughout this paper are inimical to a family's participation in school. Catholic schools are a "privilege, not a right."[346] As such, if a family is not living up to the three questions of accountability presented earlier, they may well be invited to leave the school. This is not an infrequent experience in the diocese; nor is it one without sorrow both on the part of the family as well as the pastor.[347] Wichita tells families in Catholic schools,

> The question of active stewardship is not a matter of money, but of active practice of the faith. Catholic schools are not primarily academic institutions; they are first and foremost schools of formation in faith, moral values, service, and spirituality. Our Catholic schools can succeed only if they work hand in hand with the parents. Your active stewardship in the parish is not just desirable; it is crucial to everything you and we want to accomplish for your child.[348]

Not infrequently families experience dramatic changes in their ability to give of their time, talent, and treasure. These changes tend to arise from unforeseen or even crisis type events. In such situations a family's connection to Catholic schools are not threatened. However, it is important for families to keep in constant contact with a pastor so he can understand the pressures and adjust his expectations accordingly.[349] One joy of a Catholic education provided according to this model is precisely that it can support families through various

---

[342] See Appendix D for the "Do's and Don't of Financing Schools: Legal Considerations."

[343] National Conference of Catholic Bishops, *The Rites: Volume One* (Collegeville, MN: Liturgical Press, 1990) 406.

[344] CDOWK, *Suggested Talking Points for Pastors & Catholic School Families in the Parish Grade School.*

[345] Ibid.

[346] Ibid.

[347] Some talking points for pastors in Wichita include, "As pastor: a. I have the responsibility of cultivating and forming families as active stewards. b. I am also accountable to God for being a good steward of the parish's limited financial resources. Therefore I am responsible for determining if a family is making a good faith effort at living out the Stewardship Way of Life" (ibid.)

[348] Ibid.

[349] Ibid.

trials, crises, and irregular situations. Single parent families, first generation immigrants, families suffering from job loss, families whose members have chronic illnesses, do not lose the possibility of a Catholic education for their children. Thus the common demographic of a Catholic school in Wichita is more diverse than demographics of Catholic schools based solely on tuition.[350] However, this model makes other services more difficult to provide such as education for children with moderate to severe learning disabilities or with persons who experience mental or physical disabilities. This can only be remedied by an increase of stewardship by the entire parish family. Clements summarizes,

> Catholic schools exist for two primary purposes: First, and foremost, to provide a Catholic spiritual and religious educational environment that produces young men and women who are well grounded in the Catholic faith, who choose to practice their faith throughout their lifetimes, and who are ready and willing to actively participate in their parishes and dioceses as adults. Second, to provide exemplary academic and social development programs that prepare students to become responsible, productive members of society in their homes, in their workplaces, and in their communities.[351]

As such, Catholic schools themselves seek to form disciples as stewards and commission them to be missionary in their manner of living.

United Catholic Stewardship

United Catholic Stewardship (UCS) is the title given to the unified commitment of the parishes in the Diocese of Wichita to be stewardship parishes. It is also the combined efforts of each parish to support the mission and ministry of the Diocese of Wichita as a stewardship diocese as well as the Universal Church. UCS was adopted after the 1984 the diocesan gatherings A People Gathered and Emmaus.[352] The Wichita document The Formation of Christian Stewards succinctly summarizes what UCS is:

> United in our Catholic faith, formed and responding as Christian disciples with grateful and generous hearts, individuals and families, young and old, within each parish were invited and

---

[350] Ziegler, "The State of Catholic Schools."

[351] Clements, Time, Talent, and Treasure, Kindle Locations 1106-1108.

[352] The History of Wichita cites several characteristics of UCS, "It would be Parish based; It would provide the opportunity for individuals, young and old, to experience and live out their call to discipleship, through the parish, with the added invitation and opportunity through the parish to extend this discipleship (stewardship in action) to the wider diocesan and universal church; Parishes would seek to become viable and vibrant places when they strived to identify, plan, and provide for the needs of their parishioners by establishing well organized pastoral structures and mission statements along with related goals, objectives, and action plans; Parishes would be challenged to become places of hospitality, prayer, formation, and service. And importantly, in that order; It is believed, if parishes would seriously take this role upon themselves, we could expect and experience an increase sense of parishioners gratitude, generosity, and sacrificial giving and sharing of their God given giftedness in support of the broad mission of the parish and of the wider church" (History, 2).

encouraged to recognize, receive, share and return their God-given grace and giftedness in love of God and neighbor. It was to be the desired goal within each parish to instill a sense of hospitality, prayer, formation and service by first fulfilling the mission of each parish community, and in unity to extend that generosity, gratitude and service to the diocese and to the wider needs of the universal Church. This unity in action was to:

1. Recognize, strengthen and support the role of the family in the life of the Church.
2. Stimulate and broaden local parish life, bringing about the formation and unity among parishioners as they share generously, sacrificially and proportionately their varied grace and God-given giftedness of time, talent and treasure.
3. Provide the invitation, encouragement and opportunity for all to experience, respond to and fulfill their Baptismal call to discipleship.
4. Identify, plan and provide for the needs of the parish community by establishing mission statements, related goals, objectives and action plans along with the pastoral and operational structure to facilitate, support and maintain the process.
5. Recognize the parish as the primary and ordinary recipient of the sharing of our individual and family God-given giftedness from which the parish would support its mission while also proportionately sharing and providing for the ordinary and special needs of the diocese and the wider universal Church.[353]

Among the more direct benefits of UCS are the absence of cathedraticums and second collections. These, as well as the diocesan offices, are funded by parishes giving 10% of their ordinary income to the diocese. Parishes in the Wichita metro area also pay a subsidy to the diocese to support Catholic schools of anywhere from 4% - 16%, most at 8.5%, depending on the resources of the parish. In addition to these, parishes support the *Katherine Drexel Fund* which supports parish grade schools in areas of poverty and the *Open Doors Initiative* which supports individual students from impoverished parishes who seek entry into Catholic High Schools. Thus, UCS, with its accompanying ministries, is a concrete response to the summons of Vatican II,

> Various forms of the apostolate should be encouraged, and in the whole diocese... all undertakings and organizations, be they catechetical, missionary, charitable, social, familial, educational, or anything else pursuing a pastoral aim, should be directed toward harmonious action (*Christus Dominus*, 17; AA, 10).

Among the most visible elements of the fruition of UCS are a vibrant laity, united presbyterate, commitment to Eucharistic adoration, and increased worship of the living God in Holy Sacrifice of the Mass.

In the end, a stewardship diocese is made up of parishes that are committed to stewardship. A stewardship parish is made up of parishioners that are committed to stewardship. Parishioners are committed to stewardship only insofar as their pastors promote stewardship and form parishioners in this beautiful way of life. And this life is only as beautiful as its commitment to the spirituality of giving which imitates the life of the

---

[353] Catholic Diocese of Wichita, *The Formation of Christian Stewards*, 8.

Trinity in mutual self-gift fully revealed in the incarnation and self-emptying sacrifice of Jesus Christ.

Conclusion and The Eight Fundamental Beliefs of Stewardship

So can all that has been said in this paper be succinctly simplified? Can we see the spirituality and practice of the stewardship way of life in a single snap-shot? Wichita does so in a list of eight fundamental beliefs:[354]

1. ...everything we have received is a gift from God (i.e., life, love, health, talents, family, vocation, etc.), therefore we are called to develop and share our gifts sacrificially, generously and proportionally.

2. ...stewardship is primarily about faith. It is an invitation by God for the faithful in each parish to grow in a deeper relationship with Jesus Christ.

3. ...stewardship is a spirituality that builds a way of life, expressed not in a single action or even in a number of actions but in an entire way of life. It is a committing of one's total self to the Lord.

4. ...stewardship is characterized by hospitality, prayer, formation, and service.

5. ...our bishop, pastors, and parish leaders have a crucial responsibility to live stewardship and motivate the faithful to follow their lead in order for stewardship to be a spirituality that builds a way of life.

6. ...stewardship should be integrated into all aspects of parish and diocesan mission and ministry.

7. ...the universal Church, including parish and diocesan missions, should be supported primarily by the generous, sacrificial, and proportionate sharing of time, talent, and treasure of parishioners to their parish.

8. ...we are called in scripture to return to God the first of our fruits, through our tithe.

This list forms a sort of "Magna Carta" of stewardship.[355]

In conclusion, it is said that the difference between the Sea of Galilee and the Dead Sea is that the Sea of Galilee has a river entering into it and flowing from it, whereas the Dead Sea only has a river entering it with no outlet. As a result the Sea of Galilee is teeming with life whereas the Dead Sea is a lifeless salty waste. Analogously, stewardship will be filled with vitality insofar as it is filled by the waters of discipleship and shared in the outpouring of evangelization. Without being connected to both discipleship and evangelization,

---

[354] The following list is taken from CDOWK, *Relationship*, 2. The order of the points have been changed to reflect what I consider the order of priority.

[355] Justin Clements simplifies this list of eight to a list of three: "The three fundamental principles upon which Christian stewardship is based: 1. Everything we are and have belongs to God. 2. We should be enormously grateful for all of our God-given gifts and use them responsibly. 3. Out of gratitude, we need to share a portion of our gifts of time, talent, and treasure as an expression of our discipleship in Jesus Christ" (Clements, *Time, Talent, and Treasure*, Kindle Locations 1805-1808).

stewardship in the parish setting would be like the Dead Sea – parish activities may float but they're absent of a real vitality.

Stewardship has been uniquely practiced in the Diocese of Wichita for nearly 50 years and has yielded many spiritual and material blessings. However, the passing of time has created a new situation in which the meaning and message of stewardship must be revitalized and shared anew. Stewardship is *the grateful response of a Christian disciple who recognizes and receives God's gifts and shares these gifts in love of God and neighbor.* Stewardship is an exercise of a disciple's love through the responsible care for fellow disciples in an accountable manner. It is an imitation of the interior life of the Trinity in mutual self-gift. It is a participation in the self-emptying, self-sacrificial love of Jesus Christ. It is a sharing of the Life and Love of the Holy Spirit who gives gifts and unites disciples in one communion. Stewardship is primarily concerned with the giving on one's self as a faith response to God's love. The physical and material benefits of stewardship are but symbols of this fundamental gift of self.

Let the final word be this: God is so good! Indeed, all goodness is the overflowing abundance of God's graciousness. God's abundance is a flood of giftedness that calls forth gratitude returned in self-gift. Stewardship, simply put, is a grateful response to God's abundant gifts.

BIBLIOGRAPHY

Aquinas, Thomas. *Catena Aurea: Commentary on the Four Gospels, Collected out of the Works of the Fathers: St. Matthew*. (J. H. Newman, Ed.). Oxford: John Henry Parker, 1841.

-----. *Summa Theologica.* Benzinger Brothers. ed. London: Burns Oates & Washbourne, 1947.

Arichea, D. C. & Nida, E. A. *A Handbook on the First Letter from Peter*. New York, NY: United Bible Societies, 1980.

Barry, J. D., et. al. *Faithlife Study Bible*. Bellingham, WA: Lexham Press, 2016.

Brown, Raymond E. S.S. *The Parables of the Gospels*. Glen Rock, NJ: Paulist Press, 1963.

Brown, F., et. al. *Enhanced Brown-Driver-Briggs Hebrew and English Lexicon*. Oxford: Clarendon Press, 1977.

Cantalamessa, Raniero. *Intoxicating Power of the Spirit*. Collegeville, IN: Liturgical Press, 1994.

Catholic Church. "Ad Gentes (AG): On the Mission Activity of the Church," in *Vatican II Documents*. Vatican City: Libreria Editrice Vaticana, 2011.

-----. "Apostolicam Actuostatem (AA): Decree on the Apostolate of the Laity," in *Vatican II Documents*. Vatican City: Libreria Editrice Vaticana, 2011.

-----. *Catechism of the Catholic Church* (2nd ed.). Washington, DC: United States Catholic Conference, 2000.

-----. "Christus Dominus (CD): Decree concerning the Pastoral Office of the Bishops in the Church," in *Vatican II Documents*. Vatican City: Libreria Editrice Vaticana, 2011.

-----. *Code of Canon Law: New English Translation*. Washington, DC: Canon Law Society of America, 1998.

-----. "Dei Verbum (DV): Dogmatic Constitution on Divine Revelation," in *Vatican II Documents*. Vatican City: Libreria Editrice Vaticana, 2011.

-----. "Gaudium et Spes (GS): Pastoral Constitution on the Church in the Modern World," in *Vatican II Documents*. Vatican City: Libreria Editrice Vaticana, 2011.

-----. "Lumen Gentium (LG): Dogmatic Constitution on the Church," in *Vatican II Documents*." Vatican City: Libreria Editrice Vaticana, 2011.

-----. "Presbyterorum Ordinis (PO): Decree on the Ministry and Life of Priests," in *Vatican II Documents.* Vatican
City: Libreria Editrice Vaticana, 2011.

-----. *The Roman Missal: Renewed by Decree of the Most Holy Second Ecumenical Council of the Vatican,*
Promulgated by Authority of Pope Paul VI and Revised at the Direction of Pope John Paul II (Third Typical
Edition). Washington D.C.: United States Conference of Catholic Bishops, 2011.

-----. "Sacrosanctum Concilium (SC): Constitution on the Sacred Liturgy. In *Vatican II Documents,*" in *Vatican II*
Documents. Vatican City: Libreria Editrice Vaticana, 2011.

Catholic Diocese of Wichita. *Characteristics of a Christian Steward.* Wichita, KS: Catholic Diocese of Wichita,
1999, Accessed August 9th, 2017, http://catholicdioceseofwichita.org/office-of-
stewardship/documents/the-four-pillars-of-parish-stewardship-1/282-characteristics-of-a-christian-
steward-1/file.

-----. *Characteristics of a Stewardship Parish in the Catholic Diocese of Wichita.* Wichita, KS: Catholic Diocese of
Wichita, 1997.

-----. *Do's and Don'ts of Financing Schools: Legal Considerations.* Wichita, KS: Catholic Diocese of Wichita, circa
2008.

-----. *The Formation of Christian Stewards: A Parish Stewardship Council Handbook.* Wichita, KS: Catholic
Diocese of Wichita, June 2009, accessed August 1, 2017, http://catholicdioceseofwichita.org/office-of-
stewardship/documents/council-resources-1/284-parish-stewardship-council-handbook-1/file.

-----. *The History of Stewardship in the Diocese of Wichita.* Wichita, KS: Catholic Diocese of Wichita, date
unknown, accessed July 14, 2017, http://catholicdioceseofwichita.org/stewardship-
resources/documents/history-of-stewardship-1/5221-history-of-stewardship-in-the-diocese-of-wichita-
1/file.

-----. *The Pillars of Parish Stewardship.* Wichita, KS: Catholic Diocese of Wichita, 2004, accessed August 9th,
2017, http://catholicdioceseofwichita.org/office-of-stewardship/documents/the-four-pillars-of-parish-
stewardship-1/283-pillars-of-parish-stewardship-1/file.

-----. *The Relationship Between Stewardship and Development in the Catholic Diocese of Wichita.* Wichita, KS: Catholic Diocese of Wichita, 2014, accessed August 9, 2017, http://catholicdioceseofwichita.org/office-of-stewardship/documents/5325-the-relationship-between-stewardship-development-in-the-catholic-diocese-of-wichita-1/file.

-----. *Stewarding our Gifts: Annual Parish Stewardship Renewal Planning Guide 2016/2017.* Wichita, KS: Catholic Diocese of Wichita, 2016, accessed August 1, 2017, http://catholicdioceseofwichita.org/office-of-stewardship/documents/2016-2017-annual-parish-stewardship-renewal/6556-annual-parish-stewardship-renewal-planning-guide-2016-2017/file.

-----. *Suggested Talking Points for Pastors & Catholic School Families in the Parish Grade School.* Wichita, KS: Catholic Diocese of Wichita, circa 2014.

-----. *Tithing. An Act of Worship. An Act of Stewardship.* Wichita, KS: Catholic Diocese of Wichita, accessed February 26th, 2015, http://catholicdioceseofwichita.org/office-of-stewardship/documents/6172-tithing-booklet-2016/file.

Holmes, Michael W. trans. and ed. *The Apostolic Fathers in English, 3rd ed.* (Grand Rapids: Baker, 2006).

Chautard, Dom Jean-Baptiste. *The Soul of the Apostolate* (Trans. A Monk of Our Lady of Gethsemane) Charlotte, NC: TAN Books, 1946.

Clark, Stephen. *Charismatic Spirituality: The Work of the Holy Spirit in Scripture and Practice.* Cincinnati, OH: St. Anthony Messenger Press, 2004.

-----. *Christian Tithing*. East Lansing, MI: The Sword of the Spirit, 2006.

Clements, C Justin. *Time, Talent, and Treasure: Reflections on the U.S. Bishops' Model for Parish Stewardship.* Ligouri, MO: Ligouri Publications, 2006. Kindle Edition.

Copeland, Larry. "Life expectancy in the USA his a record high." *USA Today.* Oct 8th, 2014, accessed 8, 11, 2017, https://www.usatoday.com/story/news/nation/2014/10/08/us-life-expectancy-hits-record-high/16874039/.

Dulles, Cardinal Avery. "The Charism of the New Evangelizer" in Retrieving Charisms for the Twenty-First

Century. Collegeville, IN: The Liturgical Press, 1999.

Letter to Diognetus. *The Christians in the World* (prepared by the Spiritual Theology Department of the

Pontifical University of the Holy Cross). Nn. 5-6; Funk, 397-401, accessed August 8, 2017,

http://www.vatican.va/spirit/documents/spirit_20010522_diogneto_en.html.

Gardner, Howard. *Frames of Mind: The Theory of Multiple Intelligences.* New York, NY: Basic Books, 1983.

Gavigan, James; McCarthy, Brian; McGovern, Thomas (Eds.). *Saint Matthew's Gospel.* New York, NY: Four

Courts Press, 2005.

Gerber, Most Rev. Eugene J. E-mail Interview, July 19, 2017.

-----. Phone Interview, July 25, 2017.

-----. "Human Love in the Divine Plan." Paper presented at the Diocesan Stewardship Conference in the Diocese

of Cheyenne, Wyoming, January 18-20, 2005.

-----. *"A Bishop's Journey to Stewardship."* Paper presented at the annual International Catholic Stewardship

Conference, Toronto, Canada, October 28th, 2002.

Ginns, R. "The Gospel of Jesus Christ according to St Luke," in *A Catholic Commentary on Holy Scripture*. Eds.

Bernard Orchard and Edmund Sutcliffe. New York, NY: Thomas Nelson, 1953.

Hahn, Scott. *Evangelizing Catholics: A Mission Manual for the New Evangelization.* Huntington, IN.: Our Sunday

Visitor, 2014.

Hamm, Dennis. *Philippians, Colossians, Philemon*. Eds. Peter. S. Williamson and Mary Healy Grand Rapids, MI:

Baker Academic, 2013.

Hemberger, Msgr. Robert. *A History of Stewardship in the Diocese of Wichita*. Wichita: Catholic Diocese of

Wichita, circa 2003. Audio.

Holet, Fr. Robert, DMin. *The First and the Finest: Orthodox Christian Stewardship as Sacred Offering.*

Bloomington, IN: Author House, 2013.

Hultgren, Arland J. *The Parables of Jesus: A Commentary.* Cambridge: Eerdmans Publishing Co., 2000.

Jackels, Most Rev. Michael O., "The Spirituality of Stewardship: A Holy Exchange of Gifts," YouTube video, 3:24, posted by the Catholic Diocese of Wichita, April 2, 2010, accessed August 8, 2017,

http://catholicdioceseofwichita.org/wichita-news/11480-bishop-talks-about-giving-of-self-at-mass-

11480.

Jones, A. "The Gospel of Jesus Christ according to St Matthew" in *A Catholic Commentary on Holy Scripture*.

Eds. Bernard Orchard and Edmund Sutcliffe. New York, NY: Thomas Nelson, 1953.

Keating, Daniel. *First and Second Peter, Jude*. Grand Rapids, MI: Baker Academic, 2011.

Lanzrath, Rev. John. *The Spirituality of Stewardship*. Wichita, KS: Catholic Diocese of Wichita, 2010. DVD Series.

Loicey, Lois. "Stewardship and Evangelization." Paper presented at ICSC 2015, October, 23, 2015.

Martinez, Luis. *The Sanctifier*. Paterson, NJ: St. Anthony Guild Press, 1957.

MacEvilly, John. *An Exposition of the Epistles of St. Paul and of the Catholic Epistles*. New York, NY: Benziger

Brothers, 1898.

Mallon, Fr. James. *Divine Renovation: From a Maintenance to a Missional Parish*. New London, CT: Twenty

Third Publications, 2014.

Mann, Fred. "Catholics, Mormons see most growth in Wichita and Kansas." *The Wichita Eagle*, May 7, 2012,

accessed September 1, 2016, http://www.kansas.com/news/article1091733.html.

McArdle, Deacon Donald R. *Grateful and Giving: How Msgr. Thomas McGread's Stewardship Message has

Impacted Catholic Parishes throughout the Country*. Evans, GA: Catholic Stewardship Consultants, 2011.

McGread, Msgr. Thomas. *Catholic Stewardship Consultants Blog,* accessed August 14, 2017,

http://www.catholicsteward.com/category/msgr-mcgread.

-----. "A Foundation for Stewardship," YouTube video, 8:31, posted by the Catholic Diocese of Wichita, January

27, 2017, accessed August 8, 2017, https://www.youtube.com/watch?v=jFdMyFRz3H8.

Murphy, Gabriel F.S.C. *Charisms and Church Renewal*. Rome: Catholic Book Agency, 1965.

National Conference of Catholic Bishops. *The Rites: Volume One*. Collegeville, MN: Liturgical Press,

1990.

New American Bible (Revised Edition). Washington, DC: The United States Conference of Catholic Bishops, 2011.

Pope Francis. *Meeting with Polish Bishops: Address of His Holiness Pope Francis* (given as a response to questions posed by the Polish Bishop at meeting in Krakow, July 27, 2016), accessed August 14, 2017, https://w2.vatican.va/content/francesco/en/speeches/2016/july/documents/papa-francesco_20160727_polonia-vescovi.html.

-----. *Evangelii Gaudium*. Vatican City: Libreria Editrice Vaticana, 2013.

Pope St. John Paul II. *Man and woman He created them: A Theology of the Body*, trans. M. Waldstein. Boston, MA: Pauline Books & Media, 2006.

-----. *Message of Pope John Paul II for the World Congress of Ecclesial Movements and New Communities.* Vatican City: Libreria Editrice Vaticana, 1998.

-----. *Redemptoris Mission*. Vatican City: Libreria Editrice Vaticana, 1990.

Pope Paul VI. *Evangelii Nuntiandi*. Vatican City: Libreria Editrice Vaticana, 1975.

Rath,Tom. *Strengths Finders 2.0.* New York, NY: Gallup Press, 2007.

Ratzinger, Joseph. "The Holy Spirit as *Communio*: Concerning the Relationship of Pneumatology and Spirituality in Augustine," trans. Peter Casarella. *Communio*, 25 (1998): 324–37.

Rivers, Robert. *From Maintenance to Mission*: *Evangelization and the Revitalization of the Parish*. Mahwah, NJ: Paulist Press, 2005.

Sheed, F.J. *The Confessions of St. Augustine*. New York, NY: Sheed & Ward, 1943.

Schuckman, Rev. Kenneth. "Stewardship Renewal Letter." Presented by letter to the parishioners of St. Mary's Newton, KS, 1997.

Smail, Tom. *The Giving Gift: The Holy Spirit in Person.* London: Hodder & Stoughton, 1988.

St. Francis of Assisi Parish. *Parish Family Agreement*. Wichita, KS: Catholic Diocese of Wichita, 2016. Accessed 8, 12, 2017.

-----. *Stewardship: Living Life as God Intended It*. Wichita, KS: St. Francis of Assisi Parish, 2004.

-----. 2017 *Stewardship Time and Talent Adult Form*. Wichita, KS: Catholic Diocese of Wichita, 2017. Accessed August 2, 2017.

http://www.stfranciswichita.com/SFA/media/pdfs/church/stewardship/2017_stewardship_time_talent _adult.pdf.

-----. *2017 Stewardship Time and Talent Grades 6-8 in 2017-2018*. Wichita, KS: Catholic Diocese of Wichita, 2017. Accessed August 2, 2017. ht http://www.stfranciswichita.com/SFA/media/pdfs/church/stewardship/2017_stewardship_time_talent _youth_6_8.pdf.

-----. *2017 Stewardship Time and Talent Grades 9-12 in 2017-2018*. Wichita: Catholic Diocese of Wichita, 2017, accessed August 2, 2017, http://www.stfranciswichita.com/SFA/media/pdfs/church/stewardship/2017_stewardship_time_talent _youth_9_12.pdf.

Stegman, T. D. *Second Corinthians*. Grand Rapids, MI: Baker Academic, 2009.

Swanson, James. *Dictionary of Biblical Languages with Semantic Domains: Greek* (New Testament). Electronic ed. Oak Harbor: Logos Research Systems, 1997.

Logos Bible Software 5.2a SR-7 (5.2.1.0171). *The English-Hebrew Reverse Interlinear Old Testament New Revised Standard Version,* 2014.

United States Conference of Catholic Bishops. *Go and Make Disciples: A National Plan and Strategy for Catholic Evangelization in the United States.* Kindle edition. Washington, D.C.: United States Conference of Catholic Bishops, 2002.

-----. *Stewardship: A Disciple's Response: A Pastoral Letter on Stewardship. Tenth Anniversary Edition.* Includes *To Be a Christian Steward: A Summary of the U.S. Bishops' Pastoral Letter on Stewardship* and *Stewardship and Development in Catholic Dioceses and Parishes: a Resource Manual.* Washington, D.C.: United States Conference of Catholic Bishops, 2002.

-----. *Stewardship and Young Adults.* Washington D.C.: USCCB, 2003.

-----. *Stewardship and Teenagers.* Washington D.C.: USCCB, 2007.

Vanhaverbeke, Rev. Kenneth. *"Go and See" Workbook: Practical Ideas of How to Increase Stewardship*

Participation in the Parish and the History of Stewardship in the Diocese of Wichita. Wichita, KS: Catholic Diocese of Wichita, 2012.

Weddel, Sherry. *Forming Intentional Disciples: The Path to Knowing and Following Jesus.* Kindle Edition. Huntington, IN: Our Sunday Visitor, 2012.

Welliver, Tracey Earl. *Everyday Stewardship: Reflections for the Journey*. New Berlin, NJ: Liturgical Publications, 2015.

Williamson, Peter S. "Charisms" in *New Catholic Encyclopedia*. Electronic ed. 2010 supplement.

-----. *Vision of Ideal Parish in Light of the Paradigm of the Apostolic Church*. Ann Arbor, MI: self-published, 2016.

Wooten, Cindy. *"Pope says laypeople share responsibility for church."* *Catholic News Service,* August 23, 2012, accessed July 25, 2017, http://www.catholicnews.com/services/englishnews/2012/pope-says-laypeople-share-responsibility-for-church.cfm.

Zech, Charles E. *Best Practices in Parish Stewardship*. Huntington, IN: Our Sunday Visitor, 2008.

Ziegler, J.J. "The State of Catholic Schools in the US." *The Catholic World Report*. May 31, 2011, accessed August 14, 2017, http://www.catholicworldreport.com/2011/05/31/the-state-of-catholic-schools-in-the-us/.

APPENDICES

Appendix A – A List of Parables in the New Testament

The following pages are taken directly from Fr. Raymond E. Brown's book *The Parables of the Gospels*, pages 25-28. It has been retyped here to avoid a photo copy. The only addition is the numbering of the parables on the left hand column. The numbers represent the passages considered as parables by Arland J. Hultgren in *The Parables of Jesus: A Commentary*. The lines in bold are the parables I consider to be directly related to stewardship.

(A) Similitude: short similes or metaphors which illustrate, by means of the characteristics of the things, persons or actions described.

	Title	Mark	Matthew	Luke	John
	Physician and the Sick	2:17	9:12	5:31	
	Wedding Guests and the Bridegroom	2:19-20	9:14-15	5:34-35	
1	*Patch	(2:21)	9:16	5:35	
2	*Wineskin	(2:22)	9:17	5:37-39	
3	*Divided Kingdom & Divided House	3:24-26	12:25-26	11:17-18	
4	*Strong Man	3:27	12:29	11:21-22	
	Salting with Fire	(9:49)			
	Salt Losing Its Savor	(9:50a)	(5:13	12:34-35	
	Salt Within	(9:50b)			
	City on a Hill		(5:14)		
	Lamp on a Lampstand	4:30-32	(5:14-15)	8:16; 11:33	
5	***Mustard Seed**	**4:30-32**	**(13:31-32)**	**13:18-19**	
6	***Leaven**		**(13:33)**		
	Sheep without a Shepherd	6:34	9:36		
	Leaven of the Pharisees	8:15	16:6-11		
7	***Budding Fig Tree**	**13:28-29**	**24:32-33**	**21:29-31**	
	Treasure in Heaven		6:19-21	12:33-34	
	Eye, Lamp of the Body		6:22-23	11:34-36	
	Birds of the Air/Ravens		6:26	12:24	
	Sparrows			12:6-7	
	Lillies of the Field		6:28-30	12:27-28	
8	**Son Asking His Father**		**7:9-11**	**11:11-13**	
	Wolves in Sheep's Clothing		(7:15)		
	Tree Known by It's Fruit		(7:16-20)	6:43-44	
9	**House Built on Rock**		7:24-27	6:47-49	
	Plentiful Harvest, Few Laborers		9:37-38	(10:2)	

	Mark	Matthew	Luke
Sheep Among Wolves		(10:16)	(10:3)
Wise as Serpents; Innocent as Doves		(10:16)	
Outside of the Cup		23:25-26	11:39-41
Whited Sepulchers		23:27	11:44
Hen Gathering Brood		23:37	13:34
Lightning		24:27	17:24
The Body and the Vultures		24:28	17:37
Herod the Fox			13:32

(B) Vignette: illustration which consists in an animated picture

#		Mark	Matthew	Luke
	Winnowing Fan		**3:12**	**3:17**
	Defendant		5:25-26	12:58-59
	Beam in the Eye		7:3-5	6:41-42
	Narrow Gate/Door		7:13-14	13:23-24
10	Children Playing		11:16-19	7:31-35
	Empty House		12:43-45	11:24-26
11	*Sower	4:1-20	13:1-23	8:4-15
12	*Seed Growing by Itself	4:26-29		
13	*Weeds and the Wheat		13:24-30; 36-42	
14	*Treasure in the Field		13:44	
15	*Merchant and the Pearl		13:45	
16	*Fishers and the Net		13:47-50	
17	*Householder		13:52	
18	*Lost Sheep		18:10-14	(15:3-7)
19	Lost Coin			(15:8-10)
20	*Two Sons		21:28-32	(7:29-30)
	Gnat and Camel		23:24	
21	Watchful Doorkeeper/Servants	13:34-37		(12:35-38)
22	*Thief in the Night		24:43-44	(12:39-40)
23	Servant in the Master's Absence		24:45-51	(12:42-46)
	Servant and the Master's Will			(12:47-48)
24	Ten Virgins		25:1-12	(13:25)
25	Judgment on the Sheep and Goats		25:31-46	(13:26-27)
	Axe at the Tree Root			3:9
26	Two Debtors			7:40-43
27	Importuning Friend			11:5-8
28	*Rich Fool			12:16-21
29	*Barren Fig Tree			13:6-9
30	*Last Place at Table			14:7-11
	Poor Guests			14:12-14
31	Tower Builder			14:28-30
32	Warring King			14:31-32

33	Shrewd (Dishonest) Steward	16:1-8
34	Master and the Servants	17:7-10
35	*Corrupt Judge	18:1-8
36	*Pharisee and Publican	18:9-15

(C) Narrative: a full scale story used to illustrate.

37	*Tenants in the Vineyard	12:1-11	21:33-43	20:9-18	
38	*(Wedding) Feast/Banquet		22:1-10	14:16-24	
39	*King's Vengeance		22:3, 6-7		
40	*Wedding Garment		22:11-14		
41	*Talents/Pounds		25:14-30	19:11-26	
42	*King and His Subjects			19:12, 14, 27	
43	Unmerciful Servant		18:23-35		
44	Laborers in the Vineyard		20:1-15		
45	Good Samaritan			10:29-37	
46	Prodigal Son (Forgiving Father			15:11-32	
47	Lazarus			16:19-31	

(D) Proverbs, Riddles, Miscellaneous

48	*Physician Heal Yourself			(4:23)	
	Prophet in His Own Country	6:4	13:57	(4:24)	4:44
49	*Interior Defilement	7:14-23	(15:10-11; 15-20)		
50	*Blind Leading the Blind		15:14	6:39	
	Disciple and Teacher		10:24-25	(6:40)	13:16
51	*Old Wine			5:39	
	Faithfulness			(16:10, 11-12)	
	Serving Two Masters		6:24	(16:13)	
	Carcass and the Vultures		24:28	17:17	

Appendix B - Seven Things the Catholic Church Can do to Increase Contributions

(Taken from Zech, *Why Catholics Don't Give*, 127-135)

1. Build Community: If parishioners don't feel a sense of community, the parish shouldn't bother with stewardship. It won't take hold... The parish needs to find every opportunity to build a sense of community.

2. Give Parishioners a Role in Parish Decision-Making Processes: Parishioners want more say about how their parishes are run... They want to be consulted and have direct input into decision-making processes. In parish financial matters they expect accountability and transparency.

3. Develop Stewardship: This is not only a practical solution, with enormous financial benefits, it is also mission-driven and theologically sound. In fact, stewardship is so much a part of the mission of the Church, so theologically sound, that it probably should be emphasized even if the Church wasn't interested in raising more money. The emphasis on the time and talent dimensions are at least as critical as the emphasis on treasure.

4. Minimize the Use of 'Volunteers': It is important to impress upon our parishioners that the time and talent they contribute should be viewed as 'ministry,' not merely 'volunteer' activity.

5. Institute Pledging.

6. Meet the Special Needs of Parishioners.

7. Remind Parishioners that Contributing Through Estate Planning is Good Stewardship.

Appendix C: Best and Worst Practices for Stewardship Renewal

Best Practices for Stewardship Renewal

(Taken from Catholic Diocese of Wichita, *Formation*, 21-30):

- Clear vision and mission statement
- Bulletin inserts
- Stewardship brochures
- Parish newsletter: parish events and activities; stewardship messages
- Stewardship council
- Leadership retreats
- Parish ministry directory/booklet,
- Lay witness presentations
- Welcoming committee
- Registering new parishioners
- New parishioner receptions
- Ministry fairs
- Parish dinner
- Annual parish stewardship renewal
- Time and Talent Commitment forms
- Appreciation
- Accountability
- Parish pastoral plan
- Periodic surveys
- Parish mission
- Home visits

Worst Practices: 10 key mistakes to avoid:

(Taken from McGread, Blog, June 10, 2010)

- Too many stewardship Sundays: "stewardship fatigue" is a reality, so at some point you have to conclude the renewal, even if the response is not what you'd hoped for.
- Conflicting events/ announcements during your stewardship Sunday
- Lay witness is off-message: your lay witness speakers shouldn't preach about the meaning of stewardship, but rather, simply share how they have practiced stewardship in their lives.
- Allowing sign-up sheets during your ministry fair: don't do this! The problem with this method is that it does not provide any accountability. The solution is to have interested parishioners sign up on a *commitment card* instead.
- Separating time & talent from treasure
- Poor "build up" to commitment Sunday: it needs to be clear that commitment Sunday is the "big day."

- An uninspiring commitment Sunday: teams of parishioners should be handing out commitment cards at the doors of the church. The pastor should preach at all masses, and the homily should be 100% about stewardship. It should be an inspiring call to action.
- No follow-up announcements
- Poor ministry follow-up: not following up with parishioners who have signed up for a ministry has been called "stewardship suicide."
- Lacking a spiritual focus: above all, it needs to be a time of spiritual conversion, in which parishioners respond joyfully, with gratitude to god, by investing themselves in the faith community."

Appendix D -Do's and Don'ts of Financing Schools: Legal Considerations

Dos:

- Incorporate an expectation of active stewardship into all parish activities, not just schools: for example, sacramental preparation, parish religious education, use of facilities, serving in leadership, serving in ministries.

- Review enrollment status on the basis of active stewardship. Consider attendance at Sunday Mass, regular participation in the sacraments, participation in religious education, service to parish ministries, and public support for church teaching, as well as making and keeping a good faith tithing pledge.

- Invite all parish members to complete an annual stewardship commitment of time, talent, and treasure.

- When giving records are reviewed, review all families who have pledged. For example, send letters to all families who are not current, not just school families.

- If your parish has or wants to have a "tithing policy," have it reviewed by the Chancery or diocesan counsel.

Don'ts:

- Do not specify an amount that a family must contribute to ensure admission to school, or otherwise "tie" a family's financial contribution to enrollment.

- Do not allow parishioners to choose between making contributions to the parish or paying the actual cost of education (i.e. tuition).

- Do not deny admission to a student on the sole basis that the parents do not make a financial contribution to the parish.

- Do not apply more pressure to school parents to tithe than others in the parish.

- Do not review only the financial giving of school parents.

- Do not compare the amount parents tithe to the parish to the actual cost of their children's education.

- Do not ask to review the parishioner's tax returns; to do so negates the notion of gift.

ABOUT THE AUTHOR

 Fr. Jarrod Lies (pronounced "Lease") is the son of David and Patty Lies. On May 26th, 2001 he was ordained by Bishop Gerber to the Diocese of Wichita, Kansas. He holds undergraduate degrees in Philosophy and Theology from Conception Seminary College and Master's degrees in Scripture and Divinity from the Pontifical College Josephinum. In 2018 Fr. Jarrod completed a License in Sacred Theology for the New Evangelization through Sacred Heart Seminary in Detroit, MI.

2001 – 2003 –   Parochial Vicar, Pittsburg, Kansas, at Our Lady of Lourdes Parish

2003 – 2011 -   Director of Pastoral Care (chaplain) at Bishop Carroll Catholic High School.

2007 – 2012 –   Main Celebrant of Extraordinary Form at St. Anthony's Catholic Church in Wichita.

2008 – 2015 -   Pastor of St. John's, Clonmel, KS, a rural parish of 160 families.

2011 – 2015 -   Director of the Office of Faith Formation for the Diocese of Wichita

2015 –   Pastor of St. Francis of Assisi parish in Wichita, KS. St. Francis, a parish of 2700 families.

More content from Fr. Jarrod can be found under "Pastor's Corner" at www.stfranciswichita.com.